Another
101 Tales of a Middle-Class
Middle-Child

By Pete Zakroff

Edited by Terry Zakroff and Herb Levin

Artwork by Laura Tempest Zakroff

Another 101 Tales of a Middle-Class Middle-Child

Special thanks to my wife, Terry, and our children, Stephen, Dennis, and Laura for their comments, suggestions and support. I'd also like to thank my sister, Elizabeth Doucet Goldman, Marcy Altimano, and Herb Levin for their efforts in helping to bring this latest book to life, as well as all the characters I've met from kindergarten through retirement who provided me with much of the content for the tales in this tome.

Introduction

Years ago, a late friend, Ron Zucca, offered to set me up with an audience and just have me talk. He felt I could speak about lessons-learned and humorous experiences that many folks born in the late forties through the early sixties could relate to. Sadly, Ron died before we could put this show together. As a result, the idea was put on the shelf for several years.

However, the COVID-19 pandemic in 2020 gave me an opportunity to write about my experiences rather than present them to a live audience. When I began assembling my first group of essays, I reached 25 with no problems. At 25 I realized I had many more adventures I wanted to cover. When the total reached 50, I again knew there was more I wanted to present. I continued writing until I reached 101. Upon reaching that number I decided to publish what I had. The result, released in September of 2020, became "101 Tales of a Middle-Class Middle Child."

Once the book was published, I continued collecting memories from my past experiences, including growing up in Philadelphia and living in South Jersey. I also scripted some of my favorite business experiences, recalled time spent in South Carolina, as well as classic stories and people from Ocean City, New Jersey. To round out the new effort I provided additional stories about growing old and the wonders of modern medicine. This new publication, "Another 101 Tales of a Middle-Class Middle Child" provides added details about my life and family, as well as the many things that made me "Pete."

Chapter 1: Philly on My Mind

After reading my first book, *101 Tales of A Middle-Class, Middle-Child*, a childhood friend, Herb Levin, remarked, "We were really lucky growing up in the 1950's and 1960's. It was a great time!" I had to agree with him based on the fond memories I have of those years.

West Oak Lane Memories

It was a simple and fun time growing up in West Oak Lane. There were so many things kids today will never experience. For example, every spring a photographer would come down the street walking a brown and white pony and carrying western gear. For a few dollars you could have your picture taken as a cowboy and receive a color 5 x 7 print a few days later.

Several days a week a milkman in a white uniform delivered fresh milk in glass bottles to our house. Sometimes he stopped by later with half gallons of ice cream for sale as well as other dairy products. There were weekly visits by the Bond Bread Man with his large tray full of boxed glazed donuts, loaves of fresh, brightly packaged Bond Bread, cookies, cakes, and Danish rings.

If the breadman didn't have what tickled my fancy, I could always walk around the corner to Al's at 69th and Ogontz and get a Tastykake. In the 50's and 60's they were twice the size of those sold today and only cost fifteen cents.

If we wanted homemade ice cream, all we had to do was walk one block north up Ogontz to Andrews Avenue, where on the corner there was Pflaumer's, a family-owned ice cream parlor. They didn't offer 101 flavors, but what they made was delicious.

On Saturday mornings, at the age of ten, my friend Bob Stein, a future cardiologist, and I would take the Number 6

Trolley to Broad and Olney and then grab a bus down to 5th street to the Steiner School of Art for oil painting lessons. That's where I learned to paint sailing ships and landscapes. I also learned that oil paint takes a while to dry.

Between the ages of 8 and 10, many of us were proud members of Cub Scout Pack 132, Den 3. Our Den included Michael Derowitz, a tall red-headed kid, David Goldstein, Jerry Litvin, Herb Levin, and Bob Stein. Herb and Michael's moms were our den mothers. We were sponsored by Ezrath Israel, a conservative synagogue at 69th and Ogontz Avenues. I fondly remember an arts and crafts session in the basement of Bob Stein's house, where his father guided us in making colorful Indian war shields from cardboard. I can still see the famous depiction of Custer's Last Stand Bob's dad, Harry, had hanging on the wall.

Some things just stick with me from those early days of my youth. I can coldly remember an overnight scouting trip in February at the Briar Woods campground out on Old York Road, in Cheltenham, where we spent the night in pup tents. It still sends a chill up my spine. And, if we were making a fire, older scouts would send us out on a wild goose chase looking for a left-handed smoke shifter, something that didn't really exist.

Then, when I joined the Boy Scouts, Troop 241, we spent a weekend at Treasure Island, a scouting site on the Delaware river. Here again our outing was in the middle of winter. What makes the memory so strong is the fact that someone left the eggs outside overnight and they froze solid. Do you know how hard it is to peel frozen eggs if you want to cook them for breakfast?

And who could forget Memorial Day? In the morning we would decorate our two-wheelers with red, white, and blue crepe paper, then ride up to the Philadelphia National Cemetery just several blocks away at Haines St. and Limekiln Pike to watch the military ceremony honoring soldiers interred there from the Civil War and later conflicts.

Sunday afternoons were special in the spring and fall. If it was a bright, warm day, my father would ask if we wanted to go to Valley Green and feed the ducks. Valley Green along the Wissahickon Creek was a beautiful place to be on one of those days and it was less than 30 minutes away. You could take off your shoes and wade into the creek, feed the ducks, or catch crayfish that swam along the creek's edge. They were easy to catch, but never lasted long in the fish tank at home. And, if we were good, my father would treat us to ice cream at the Valley Green Inn. I still have a painting of that classic place hanging on my wall.

Years later, as a teenager, it was also a great make out spot on Friday nights. There were plenty of places to park near the entrance. And, if we kept our motors running, the police didn't usually bother us.

West Oak Lane was definitely a great place to live and grow up in Philly during the 50's and early 60's.

Great Philly Places of the Past

Growing up in Philly introduced me to a great number of places that no longer exist except in my memories. When my siblings and I would go to our father's office at 341 North Third Street on Saturday mornings to sweep the floors and allow him to check the mail, sometimes on the way home we would stop at a place called Johnson's Fair. It was a big military surplus store. There we would get military green satchels to use as school bags and combat boots to wear to school in foul weather.

My father also had a warehouse at Germantown Ave. and Berks Street in North Philly. It was across the street from the original Stetson Hat company. You know the kind of hats that many cowboys wore. In fact, my dad was buried with one, though he wasn't really a cowpoke.

Just up the street from the warehouse on the 1700 hundred block of Germantown Avenue was Gaul's Chocolates, a great candy store. They made their own and boy, were they good! It was a place that made dentists happy. For years, at holiday times, like Christmas and Easter, customers were lined up down the block to pick up their orders of some of the best chocolate treats in the world.

Today, when you see ten people on the street, at least a few of them are wearing jeans like Wrangler or Levis. However, before every clothing store from Kohl's to Macy's began carrying blue jeans, one of the only places in Philly you could get them was at Rodeo Ben's on North Broad Street.

He carried western wear and a wide selection of jeans, shirts, and cowboy boots.

A few other places that were hard to forget included the Samuel Sandler Company just south of South Street in Philly. They made the best kosher salami in the business. I remember walking through there with one of my aunts at a young age and will never forget the experience or the smell.

Talking about good eats, one other place that brings back fond memories was Gino's near Willow Grove Park. During my college days at Temple, many of us would meet there on a Friday night for giant steak sandwiches which put many of those lauded steak sandwich places in South Philly to shame. For five bucks you could get one of these monster sandwiches and a large soda.

My First Phillies' Game

Being born and raised in Philly it's tough not to be or not to have been a Phillies fan at least sometime in your life. I think it started for me in 1954. I was about nine years old at the time when my father took my sister, Betsy, my brother, Rob, and myself to our first Phillies game at Connie Mack Stadium on Leigh Avenue. This was years before they built Veterans Stadium or Citizens Bank Park in South Philadelphia.

It was a night game and my father got us to the stadium early, very early, at least an hour before the start of the game. Since we didn't have dinner beforehand, he bought a Foremost Hot Dog for each of us, and two for himself. Yep, in those days the stadium served kosher hot dogs to its patrons, and they were only 25 cents each.

However, it didn't take long for three kids to finish their food. So, we sat and waited as we had nothing much else to do. Then, as the starting pitchers warmed up, my father said, "Let's go!" He wasn't a patient man and had had enough. So, we left, before the first pitch was ever thrown.

Every Kid Needs a Pet

Every kid needs a pet at some time in their lives. The first real pet we had as kids was a German Shepherd pup named Rex. Rex was brown and black and very rambunctious. According to my sister, Betsy, we got him from our Aunt Lil and Uncle Abe who lived in the second-floor apartment of a house up the street from us on Georgian Road. The problem was, we were too young and didn't really know how to care for a pet, let alone an excitable puppy. On top of that, our mom was being treated for breast cancer at the time and unable to help us. Before long, Rex went back to the aunt and uncle.

For some years after that, our only pets were goldfish, turtles, and guppies. When the goldfish and turtles passed, they would either be flushed down the toilet or buried in the back yard for fertilizer in cigar boxes. As for the guppies, they would sit on a shelf near the dining room window where we watched them swim around and reproduce like rabbits.

One Easter, our parents gave us two baby chicks and a duckling, which was a common thing to do at the time. The chicks died after a few weeks, but the duck kept on going. Several times a week, I would walk up to the Acme supermarket three blocks away and get a bag of discarded lettuce from the produce department to feed our pet. As the duck grew larger, we built a small fenced-in area in the backyard with a large bowl in the center for the duck to swim in. When we let him out, he would follow me around. Every morning, we'd be awakened by his quacking, like he knew it was time to get up for school.

When summer arrived, and we went away to camp, the duck was given to the local milkman, who had a farm. Apparently, the duck had cooked his own goose by quacking every morning at sunrise like a rooster, which disturbed the neighbors.

The next pet or pets I had were hamsters. They were more of a business than pets. If you have two hamsters, a male, and a female, it wasn't long before you had a lot more. They, like guppies, reproduce like rabbits. For a year or two, I sold the offspring to the local pet shop who resold them. If the hamsters ever escaped from their habitat in the basement, it was a challenge to recapture them. Often, I'd be down on my hands and knees trying to catch them as they hid behind the heater or oil tank in the basement.

When my hamster phase passed, due to a glut of pets on the market, I bought a baby alligator, which was about 18 inches long. Every few days, I'd give it a bath in the upstairs bathtub. Besides telling people you had an alligator for a pet, there wasn't much to it. It's not like you could cuddle up to it or have it do tricks or bark. One day, when I brought it outside on the front lawn, I received a phone call and ran back into the house to answer it. When I returned the little bugger was gone. I couldn't find him anywhere. I always wondered if he made his way into the Philadelphia sewer system, grew to twelve feet and was the subject of a science fiction movie about the monster in the sewer.

The last pet I had who spent the months of July and August at home before I left home was a feral kitten named Fifi. I was in college at the time. One of my friend's family operated a cemetery just behind the Neshaminy Mall, just outside of Philadelphia. Apparently, there was a nest of kittens in the cemetery and this one escaped. Out of pity, I adopted the kitten as a pet.

My brother, Rob, in the meantime had a pet cat named Trixie. She was jealous of Fifi and demonstrated her mouse catching skills by bringing us live mice in her mouth. Fifi, on the other hand, was wild. One day, she escaped outside, and before we knew it, she was pregnant.

One night I woke to her having a litter of kittens on my bed. What a mess! She then tried bringing her babies into the bathroom and up into the linen closet, figuring it was a safe place. That didn't exactly thrill my father. Before you could count to ten, Fifi and her litter were at the SPCA. Within a few months, I was gone also. I got married and moved to Jersey.

Send That Kid to Camp

Growing up, my sister, brother, and I were very lucky, even though we really didn't know it at the time. Unlike other

kids in the neighborhood like Bob Stein and Jimmy
Lovenstein who spent July and August at home, our parents
sent us to summer camp for many years. I didn't know why
or think much about it at the time. It just happened and I
was happy to go. Did they just want to get me and my
siblings out of their hair or was there another reason? There
was, but I didn't find out about it until years later.

My first two years of summer camp were spent at Bob White
Day Camp. The years were 1950 and 1951. A good guess at
where the camp was located was Montgomery County, PA,
but I can't find anything to confirm it since the camp doesn't
exist today. However, I do have two pictures from those
years that establish the fact that I was there. One shows me
in a cabin with other campers. The other shows me sitting in
a circle outside at what appears to be story time. Further
proof of my attendance is an evaluation letter dated from
August 1951, stating that I was a good camper but a poor
eater who wouldn't try new foods. I also have a certificate
for being a good camper, again dated from 1951.

The summers of 1952 and 1953 were different. They were
spent at Camp Green Lane, in Green Lane, PA. Green Lane
was an overnight camp where along with my sister and
brother we spent eight weeks swimming and boating in a
lake, playing softball, basketball, and volleyball, going on
nature hikes and making arts and crafts. At night there were
often campfires down by the lake where we sang traditional
campfire songs, and counselors or other staff told us ghost
stories.

We woke up to the sound of reveille every morning, learned to make our beds, had three square meals every day and went to bed when they played taps over a loudspeaker. There were two visiting days each summer where my parents came to check on us, watch us swim, or play ball, and buy camp pictures showing us in our "formal" camp shirts and shorts, or engaged in different activities. We slept on cots with wire bases and thin mattresses in log cabin-like bunkhouses up on a hill that reminded me of barracks you often see in war movies. The boys' cabins were in line on a hill. Above them, fifty feet or so higher, were the girls' cabins.

When it came to food, if there was something I didn't like, as was often the case, there was always peanut butter, jelly, and sliced bread at the table. To document my attendance at Green Lane, I do have some group shots of my counselors and campers showing I was really there. One of my strongest memories was when a counselor tried to hypnotize me and tested it out by pricking my wrist with a pin and seeing if I felt any pain. Overall, Camp Green Lane was a good experience!

My summers from 1954-60, were spent at Camp Sholom in Collegeville, PA. I don't know why we changed camps. I don't think it was anything I did, but in any event we did. The first year, I remember, we boarded a bus in Philly at the YMHA on South Broad Street and within two hours we were at camp. Every year after that my father drove us to camp - I guess to make sure we got there. Over the next seven years that was my home for eight weeks from late June until the middle of August.

My first year at Camp Sholom was spent in a large, log-cabin type structure called "The Big House." It held 4 groups of 8-10 campers each from ages 7 to 12 years of age. Bunk 7 was the youngest, then Bunk 9, Bunk 11, and Bunk 13. I was in Bunk 13. The boys' cabins were odd numbered, and the girls' bunks were even numbered (2, 4, 6, etc.).

Sholom was a lot different than Camp Green Lane. It was larger, had more campers, and as a result some of the bunks had double decker beds to accommodate the increased number of campers. Also, Sholom had a large, stone administration building which also contained the infirmary. It had numerous athletic fields, an Olympic-sized swimming pool and a lagoon for boating where Green Lane used a lake for both. There were also evening activities such as campfires, movies, and occasional sporting events. In fact, one year, I got to see Wilt Chamberlain play the camp staff. It seems Wilt was working as a member of the kitchen staff that summer. The kitchen staff played a group of counselors and easily beat them. I don't think Wilt scored a hundred points that game, but he easily could have.

Having attended Sholom for so many years with the same campers, I still remember several of their names. There was tall and skinny Richard "Spider" Steinberg from New York who went to the Bronx School of Science, little Louie Greenberg from the Logan part of Philly. Louie died young from a car accident. Other campers included Marshall Nieren from Marple-Newtown, Wayne Cherry, a distant cousin, and Howard Karloff, my nemesis. Howard and I didn't see eye to eye so one year we put on the gloves.

There was also Harvey Goldberg, who lived several blocks from me in the city near Wagner Junior High School. Harvey became a pharmacist. One other camper I remember was Marty Goldfine from Freehold, NJ. Marty was a great swimmer and actually married a girl, Fran Friedman, he met at camp. Marty became an accountant and talk about a small world. He knew my friend Neal Cupersmith from the business world. Along that line one of my camp counselors at Sholom was a fellow named Steve Seligman. Steve was my counselor for Bunk 15. Later in life he turned out to be Neal Cupersmith's partner in an accounting firm.

Those were marvelous summers. We'd wake up each morning to the sound of reveille being played over the loudspeaker. It was followed by an announcement regarding the weather and what to wear for the day. If it was going to be a hot one, we were told to wear shorts and shorts (short pants and T-shirts).

If it was going to be cold or wet, the announcer suggested we wear longs and longs (long sleeves and long pants). Once showered and dressed, we'd walk a few hundred yards to the mess hall, raise the flag, say the pledge of allegiance, and have breakfast. Just like Green Lane, we'd have a choice of cold cereal, fruit, eggs or sometimes pancakes.

After breakfast, we'd trek back to our cabin, make our beds, and prepare for the inspection of our bunks. Things had to be neat, and our beds tightly made. Following inspection, we had a set schedule of activities for each day of the week. It could be swim instructions followed by softball or basketball, lunch, then a short rest period followed by an outdoor activity like volleyball or arts and crafts. That was generally followed by an open swim at the pool with many other campers.

We were kept busy all-day long, playing sports, taking nature hikes or creating crafts for our parents. Once in a while, we would play other camps, like Green Lane, Maribel (which turned out to be owned by my mentor Val Udell) or Rock Hill in softball or volleyball. There was also row boating and canoeing in the lagoon just off the Perkiomen Creek, as well as color war activities.

Color war took place early in August. That's where the campers were evenly divided into two teams (blue and white – the camp colors) for two weeks and we competed against each other for points in a wide range of sporting activities including swimming races, softball, capture the flag, and basketball. The final competition closed with a "Sing" where each team performed different songs adapted from popular songs and Broadway show tunes. In the end, it really didn't matter which team won as it was great fun.

As teenage boys will be boys, we went on a panty raid, where we snuck out of our cabin in the middle of night, while our counselors were sleeping and stealthily ventured into the girls' side of the camp like a group of ninjas. Quietly we traversed to the cabins several hundred yards away, and quickly gathered some feminine items off the clothes lines as trophies. We returned as quietly as we had left with our counselors none the wiser for our venture.

Summer camp also introduced me to girls. One year it was Joyce Lipschitz, a cute, freckle-faced girl from Pennsauken, NJ. During another season it was Joan Feldman from Overbrook. Then there was Barbie Pollock, the camp director's daughter. She was older than I, but I was attracted to her.

In my final year at Sholom, 1960, I won the "best all-around camper" award. It was a trophy usually given to the camper in the oldest bunk who participated in all activities, displayed trust, honesty, and good sportsmanship over the course of the summer. It was a great honor for me and an award I cherished for many years.

My next few summers were spent at summer school catching up on geometry and taking some advanced courses. However, I did have one more camp experience. During my freshman year at Temple University, 1963, I applied to be a camp counselor at Freshman Camp. It was a new student orientation experience for first year students. Even though I didn't have a high scholastic average my freshman year, I decided to apply for the project. It was held at Camp Green Lane, the site of one of my earliest camp experiences. Freshman camp was a three-day experience designed to introduce freshman students to the university. And as I found out, it was a great way to meet girls. I don't know how I made the cut as a counselor. Lucky, I guess! Students with higher averages didn't. That was my last great camp experience.

Saturdays with Ben

At the ripe old age of ten or eleven, when we weren't going to either the neighborhood movies for a Saturday matinee (either we had seen the film or it was a love story) I would gather a small group of friends, which usually included Bob Stein, from up the street, and school mates Jerry Litvin and Herb Levin, and go to the Franklin Institute for the afternoon. My father, Louie, was a member of the Institute and had books of guest tickets, which meant there was no charge for us to get in.

My father would drop us off in front of the building. He gave me a few dollars for lunch at the automat and cab fare for the trip home. When you entered the building, there was a giant statue of Ben Franklin to greet you.

There was always lots to do and see at the Institute. I always enjoyed going to the Nickelodeon, the silent movie theater in the building, showing Charlie Chaplin and Buster Keaton shorts, early westerns, plus some black and white animated cartoons. Admission was five cents.

If the timing was right, we could see an astronomy show at the Fels Planetarium and learn about the wonders of the universe. After the show, there was the famous large and beating model heart that you could walk through.

In the train museum, there were several full-sized Baldwin steam locomotives to gaze at, which moved several feet back and forth. In the same area the museum featured an amazing model train layout with electric trains running in all different directions.

There was also an air museum with replicas of famous planes, as well as a wide range of models and diverse aeronautical equipment.

My last visit to the Institute was as a teenager a few years later, on New Year's Eve. The institute sponsored an overnight stay for kids where you could tour the building and see a special presentation at the planetarium at midnight. It was a fun evening, especially if you were too young to date or didn't have one for that special night.

Remote Learning Guinea Pigs

Back in the 1950's educators were exploring the possible uses of a new medium, television, for instructional purposes. My classmates and I in junior high school became test subjects for the experiment. Twice a week, a hundred or more of us were ushered into the auditorium at Wagner Junior High School in Philadelphia to watch a series of 45-minute science presentations delivered by Zachary Bernstein.

There were no video projectors or flat screen TVs in those days. Spaced around the room were several 24-inch black and white television sets. Depending upon where you were seated, it was tough to see, let alone hear. And the lessons weren't very exciting. Mr. Bernstein's sessions reminded me of some of the opening scenes from "Ferris Bueller's Day Off." They weren't very exciting or attention grabbing, but it was an experiment. We lived through it. We didn't learn much. But they tried. Today, it's large color flat screens, projection TVs, or computers and interactive communication between the presenter and the audience. However, the results sometimes are not too different if the content is not presented in an interesting or attention-grabbing manner that learners or audiences are more accustomed to.

The Four-Dollar Day

My first paying job was at the age of fourteen. It was at Martin's Aquarium on Ogontz Avenue in the West Oak Lane section of Philly. The store was just up the street from Kresge's 5 & 10, in the Acme Shopping Center, and a few doors from Hanscom's, my favorite bakery. I had frequented Martin's many times over the previous several months as I had a 20-gallon aquarium full of tropical fish at home. All had been purchased from Martin's. My collection included several beautiful angels, guppies, black mollies, zebras, and a big catfish who did a great job of keeping the tank clean with the help of a filtering system.

Since I was familiar with the store and tropical fish, and wanted to start to earn some money, I applied for a job at the store after school one day. I spoke with the manager, Ron Thomas, and explained my knowledge of tropical fish. After telling him of my desire to work there, Ron told me to come in Saturday afternoon, and they would give me a tryout.

On Saturday, I showered, put on a clean pair of pants and a dress shirt, and reported to the store at 1:00 pm. For the next three hours I talked with customers, recommended types of fish, and scooped and bagged them.

At about 4:00 pm, as the flow of customers dwindled, the manager called me over and said they had enough help in the store until it closed. He went to the cash register and handed me four dollars and said, "Thank you." And that was it. No request for me to return as a worker on another day or the next Saturday. It was the shortest time I ever worked on a job, and I never knew why I wasn't asked back. I guess it was a harbinger of why I ended up working on my own for most of my adult life.

Summer School

Unlike the movie version of Summer School, starring Mark Harmon and a bunch of underachieving and outlandish characters like special effects horror nerds, male models, and pregnant girls, my experiences were quite different.

The first course I ever failed was freshman Algebra at Central High school in Philadelphia. That was in the Spring of 1959. I just didn't get it. My mind, the teacher, and the subject just didn't click. Even going to tutoring sessions didn't help. It was frustrating. I failed it so badly that the instructor, Mr. Stern, didn't want me to take it over in summer school, but in the fall. As luck would have it, I had a different instructor the second time around and was able to get a high enough grade to pass the course on my second try.

Though I had wanted to attend Central, I realized after one year that it was not for me and decided to transfer to Olney High School, where several of my junior high classmates were going. I handled the transfer by myself, and when the next semester began in February, I was attending Olney, the "Cathedral of Learning" at Front and Duncannon Streets.

The school was a trolley car, bus ride, and a few walking blocks away. Olney was a large, three-story high school. In its prime it held close to 4000 students and offered a wide range of educational programs including academic and commercial courses of study.

I was placed in the academic track, based on my previous grades and experience at Central. Somehow, when my grades were transferred from Central to Olney they made a mistake. Instead of Algebra 2, I was given Geometry 1 and I didn't say anything about it.

As luck would have it, I failed Geometry 1 in the spring of 1960 by a few points. I had a 65 and 69 was passing. This time I decided to go to summer school to make it up. Summer school at that time in Philly was being held at Gratz High School in North Philadelphia. To get there, I'd go down a block to 69th and Ogontz avenues, ride the Number 6 trolley car to Broad and Olney, take the subway a few stops south and then walk the several blocks to Gratz.

The course was two hours a day, five days a week, for four weeks. It provided a good review and refresher on the subject. For some reason things clicked this time around and I easily passed the course. Since my summer was basically shot, I decided to take another course to fill out the summer break.

This time it was something I enjoyed: Biology 2. The course was taught by a lady named Bessy Abramowitz who regularly taught the subject at South Philadelphia High. Mrs. Abramowitz was an experienced teacher who made the subject interesting and the sessions enjoyable, even though it was being taken in the summer. I passed the course with flying colors, but only received a "B" grade on my official transcript, because it was summer school.

Long story short, when I took Geometry 2 the next semester and trigonometry after that, without ever having Algebra 2, I aced both courses. My mind was finally in sync with the math.

The following summer, since I was not going back to camp, I decided to take a couple other courses to get ahead and make my senior year in high school easier. Like the previous year, summer classes were taught at Gratz in North Philly.

The first course I took was Spanish. I had German as a language my first two years in high school and wanted to try another. Maybe it would be a little easier. Our instructor was Mr. Sunseo. As it turned out he regularly taught the language at Olney. Mr. Sunseo was about five feet six inches tall and balding. He was a smart dresser, wore boots with large heels to make him appear taller, and always had a smile on his face. I enjoyed the course and ended up with a B on my school record.

The other course I took that summer was Physics I. This course was taught by Frank Sadker. He, too, was a teacher from Olney. However, he didn't have a very high opinion of the school administration and would often ask students this question, "Why is the school district like a stagnant pond?

The first time I heard the question I wondered why we were talking biology in a physics class. But a few students who were familiar with Mr. Sadker promptly supplied the answer, "Because the scum rises to the top." He also thought it was stupid to have students get under their desks if there was an air raid alert. Like a desk would protect you from a nuclear attack. Ah, summer school!

I Can't Stands No More

Popeye the sailor from the comics and animated cartoons was famous for taking abuse until he could no longer stand it from his arch enemy, Bluto. At that point, Popeye would rip open a can of spinach, gulp it down, and beat the living daylights out of Bluto. Not that I like spinach or have a can of it on hand at all times, I had a situation where I couldn't stand it any longer and had to take action.

It was the in the Fall of 1962. I had taken some classes in summer school to ease up my regular class schedule senior year at Olney High School and took an art class. It was one 50-minute period, five days a week. On one particular Tuesday morning the instructor was out sick, and we had a substitute, Mrs. Thomas, who was new to the school.

For some reason, the "clown" sitting behind me, William Riley, a lower classman, started kicking my chair. I politely asked him to stop. Riley kept on doing it. Once again, I asked him to stop, but he continued. I asked, "What's the matter with you?" I could see it in his eyes he was brewing for a fight.

One more time I asked him to stop but it was useless to argue. He was goading me on. Having had enough, I stood up and demanded he stop. He said, "Make me!" Riley then stood up and with a stupid smile on his face took a swing at me. I ducked and returned the favor landing a few punches on his chest. He looked surprised, so did Mrs. Thomas. Though Riley and I were about the same size, once it started, I didn't stop until he was down on the floor.

With Riley on the floor, the fight stopped. The substitute teacher, Mrs. Thomas, grabbed the wall phone and called the office. In less than two minutes, Mr. Nackoney, the school disciplinarian, was at the door. He escorted us both to his office. There I explained my side of the incident.

Looking at our school histories, he saw that I had a clean record, was a hall and gym monitor, as well as a member of the varsity soccer team. I received no punishment for the altercation. Riley on the other hand apparently had a record as a troublemaker and Mr. Nackoney was familiar with him. He received several detentions for his actions. After the incident Riley never sat close to me again.

My First Set of Wheels

My first car buying experience was in the 1960's. I was a dumb kid of 16 and went with my father to two dealerships near us on North Broad Street in Philadelphia. One sold

Chevys and the other Ramblers, an American Motors product. We looked at a Chevy II convertible and a Rambler American. For some reason, which I can't fathom to this day, I picked the Rambler. It was a four-door silver gray sedan and shaped like a box. To make it look more exciting, I added black and white racing stripes from the front of the hood to the back of the trunk and put imitation white walls on all the tires. I also had custom seat covers made for it.

Over the next few years, I literally ran the Rambler into the ground. I had a couple of accidents, one on a joy ride with friends during my senior year in high school. Luckily, no one was injured. I also had an accident one day on the way to college. It was snowing, the brakes failed, and I slid into the rear of another car. These incidents certainly didn't help when it came to my insurance rates.

I also dropped the gas tank after a rock hit the welded brace holding it in place. You really know something is wrong when you're driving along, the car suddenly stops, and you see your gas tank lying on the ground 50 yards behind you. And don't get me started talking about the leaking transmission or the broken lock on the trunk. You had to stick your finger through the hole where the lock had been to open it. This was way before remotes and inside trunk releases.

I learned a lot driving the gray ghost, mostly what not to do, and what it takes to own and take care of a car.

Oh, What a Night!

As many a Charles Shultz Snoopy comic strip begins, "It was a cold and dark night." That was true of the night I graduated from Olney High School in Philadelphia. Our high school graduation ceremony was on the evening of January 23rd, 1963. It was a cold and damp winter's night. Sleet was coming down and icing the roads. My family in attendance for the event included my father, Louie, along with my sister, Betsy, and younger brother, Rob.

I can still remember several things clearly about that night. I was in the top 10th of the class, number 25 out of 369 students. I hadn't been able to move up closer to the front due to the questionable average I received from my DAR-member history teacher, Mrs. Graeff.

During the 2-hour ceremony we sang a number of religious-themed hymns as well as heard "approved" speeches by the valedictorian, Sheldon Halpern, and the salutatorian, Jaclyn Dranoff. Sheldon went to Penn and became a real estate lawyer practicing on the west coast, while Jackie went to Temple and into education. Some of the Jewish kids at the ceremony didn't sing all the songs because they deemed it inappropriate to say Jesus Christ. To me it didn't matter. These were only songs and not my beliefs.

At the close of the ceremony, I told my friend Neal Cupersmith, I'd pick him up later and we'd go together to a graduation party being held by one of our classmates. After graduation I went to dinner with my family at the CR Club restaurant just off the Roosevelt Blvd.

By the time we finished our meal, the roads were more treacherous. My father made me promise to go home after attending a party only a few blocks from the restaurant. By making and keeping the promise to my dad, I would be unable to go to Neal's house to pick him up. Neal lived several miles away and the roads to his house, Levick Street and the Tookany Creek Parkway were hilly and as a result very slippery.

Since we didn't have cell phones or computers in those days there was no way I could contact my friend. I went to the party which wasn't that great and decided to head home after about an hour before all the roads would freeze up. On my way home, in my 62 Rambler American, I drove down Levick and slid down the hill to the parkway, narrowly missing parked cars and a tree. I then crawled up Cheltenham Avenue, past Neal's house toward my home.

I felt really bad that I hadn't picked Neal up. Apparently, he waited all night for me to come. You can't imagine how bad I felt. It took several calls over several days for him to finally talk to me again and explain what happened. Luckily our friendship withstood the event and we're still friends to this day.

A Scenic Ride to the Hospital

Years before Disneyland, Disney World, Seven Flags, and Great Adventure, growing up in Philadelphia during the 1950's and 60's we had the Willow Grove Amusement Park. As kids, we could walk down the street to 69th and Ogontz Avenue and hop on the PTC number 6 trolley car which would take us through Jenkintown and Abington and drop us off right at the park. Later, when we were able to drive, it was only a 30-minute ride.

The park featured almost every type of amusement you could imagine. There were bumper cars where you could forget your driving skills or worry about insurance if you hit another car, the high-flying and swirling Tilt-A-Whirl, the Tunnel of Love for those romantics who wanted to cuddle in the dark, the Laff in the Dark fun house, and The House of Horrors with its scary mannequins and rotating barrel at the exit. And what would an amusement park be without a Ferris wheel and a merry-go-round? They were big! The park also featured arcades with games like skee ball and there was even a miniature golf course.

If you wanted a snack or treat like a hot dog, cotton candy, ice cream or water ice, vendors were scattered throughout the park. There was even a picnic area if you brought your own food. Willow Grove Park had it all.

What I remember most about this great park were the roller coasters. If they were your passion there was the Scenic, a short fast roller coaster, the Alps, a longer and larger coaster experience, and if you dared, the Thunderbolt, with its slow, dramatic climb up the rails followed by its steep, rapid and scary descent. Often a date I had brought to the park would hold on to me tightly for dear life and scream her lungs out on the way down. That was a great feeling.

However, one such ride ended up with a week-long stay in the hospital. On a Saturday night in early spring during my first year at Temple, I took a girl from Germantown High School, Francine, to the park for a date. She didn't want to ride on the Thunderbolt. She preferred the Scenic. Apparently, on that ride, I received a wooden splinter in my left leg below the knee, which I didn't notice until a day later when the leg began to swell, and the pain became unbearable.

A house call from my physician, Dr. Bloom, resulted in a diagnosis of cellulitis. Yes, they made house calls in the 60's. He wanted me to go to the hospital immediately as the infection, if it spread, could be deadly. My father took me to the University of Pennsylvania Hospital where I spent the next week being treated with antibiotics for the illness. I made a full recovery, but missed a week of classes, which ended up affecting my grades. However, that's another tale.

Today, Willow Grove Park is gone, having closed in 1975. However, those of us who had the opportunity to go there will never forget it and the many (or most) of the experiences we enjoyed there.

The Substitute

After a summer of working at the Coatesville Record as a reporter I decided to go back to college and get my M.A. in education at Temple University. Based on that experience, I couldn't imagine spending the rest of my life as a reporter. I also knew I needed a job to make some money as I was preparing to get married the following fall.

Having heard I could make about $150 a week as a substitute teacher in Philadelphia, I signed up to be a sub with the school district. $150 a week wasn't bad at the time. Now they get that or more per day. It turned out the district had a long-term sub opening for a biology teacher at Roxborough High School. It was less than 30 minutes from my home in West Oak Lane. Since I had taken biology in college, which was much more intense than the high school version, I got the job.

It really was a great gig. Most of the students were nice, polite, and interested in learning. I taught several biology classes starting at 8:00 am in the morning. In addition to biology, I had 1-2 classes daily of basic arithmetic which I co-taught with another long-term sub, William Jackson. I was done for the day and out of the building by 2:30. This gave me enough time to get to Temple for my education classes which started at 4:00 pm. I had graduate classes 4 nights a week.

The textbook being used for Biology 1 hadn't changed much from five years earlier when I took the course myself as a high school student. Working late each night after my college classes, I was able to prepare lesson plans for the next day's lecture. When it came to tests, I built on my own experiences as a student. I created my tests on mimeograph masters, the technology in use at the time, and had the school office run off copies for each class. My tests were multiple choice and fill-ins. Though the tests were the same for each class, I'd indicate a different version letter (A, B, C, D) on the bottom of each page. I would then tell the students each version was different to cut down on cheating.

The only problem with the job was the school's vice principal, Mr. Stillman. He and I never got along well. He often held staff meetings after 2:30, which was a problem for me having to get to my classes at Temple. He was never in my corner and looked for an opportunity to replace me.

At the same time I was teaching, I was also writing magazine articles. One appeared in the Sunday Philadelphia Inquirer's "World We Live in Section." It was a full color spread based on an idea I had for teaching kids about history. It was called "Rebuilding the Past from Paper and Clay." When I came into work the next day a copy was hanging on the school bulletin board. I'm sure this didn't make Mr. Stillman happy. The article's byline listed me as a biology instructor at Roxborough.

While teaching at Roxborough, I was also taking a course in programmed instruction. The final project required you to create a programmed lesson on a topic. Building on an idea from my undergraduate days of using Sherlock Holmes and Watson to solve the Macbeth murder, I developed a programmed text using illustrations from Classic Comics. I also tested the program on several students at the school which resulted in an article in the school paper.

During my semester at Roxborough, I developed a great rapport with many of my students. They would always say "Hello, sir" when we passed in the hallway, and greet me with a smile. It reminded me of Sidney Poitier's experiences in "To Sir with Love," which appeared in theaters at about the same time.

In the end, Mr. Stillman got his revenge. At the end of the first semester, a newly certified teacher was hired to take my place. The district offered me another position at Cook Junior High School in the Olney section of Philadelphia teaching English and basic math to seventh and eighth graders. I took the position for several months and was even offered a permanent position by the principal, but it was never the same experience I enjoyed at Roxborough. Three months later I left to pursue the development of one of my creative ideas for marketing with DCA Educational Products. It was based on the article that appeared in the Inquirer several months earlier on "Rebuilding the Past from Paper and Clay."

First Flight

When people hear the phrase "First Flight," many relate it to the Wright Brothers and their excursion of about 120 feet at Kitty Hawk, North Carolina in December of 1903. My first actual flight on an airplane was from Philly to Houston in April of 1968 to attend my first audiovisual convention. I was twenty-two at the time and had taken vacation days from teaching to attend the event.

The flight out on an Eastern Airlines jet was a smooth ride. It was a beautiful day. The sky was blue with hardly a cloud in the sky. This gave me a false sense of confidence about flying since I had never been on a commercial airliner before. However, I believe we had a real cowboy for a pilot on the return trip and he was practicing bull or bronco riding.

All the way back to Philly we were going up and down, down and up, and from side to side during the entire flight. I could feel my stomach churning with every dip. At one point, I made my way to the lavatory at the back of the plane and closed the door. Looking in the mirror, I could see I was an interesting shade of green. I slowly returned to my seat, holding on the arms of the seats in the aisle as I passed. Could I finish the flight without resorting to the barf bag in my seat pocket? If I needed to use it, that would be embarrassing.

Somehow, I managed not to use the bag. When we finally landed, I literally kissed the ground after exiting the plane. That also dashed any thoughts of taking flying lessons.

We've Been Robbed

By the late 1960's our West Oak Lane neighborhood had changed. As a result of "The great white flight," most of the neighbors were African American. We were one of the few white families still living on Georgian Road, a small street between 69th and Andrews Avenues, just off Ogontz. My family had been living on Georgian all my life and my father was in no mind to move as he was still living in the 1950's after my mother's passing several years earlier

At the same time, my sister, Betsy, the war correspondent, had returned to the USA and was in the middle of a divorce from her first husband, Dirck, a photographer with United Press International (UPI). She and her two dogs moved in with us on Georgian road for several months.

One night, in early fall, robbers came in through a front porch window and stole a 19-inch black and white television sitting on a table in the living room and cleaned out the freezer of frozen meats and vegetables. I guess those were the only things of value they could find downstairs.

I was amazed that during that night my sister's two dogs didn't hear them or even bark. Of course, we called the police in the morning to report the intrusion, but they never found the perpetrators. Based on that experience, my father would always keep a large hunting knife in his bedroom and sleep lightly. If after that event we came in late, Louie would come partially down the upstairs steps and yell out "Who's there?" I, on the other hand, learned to never leave anything valuable out at night when we went to bed, to make sure all the doors and windows were locked, and to turn on the alarm.

When Britannica Ruled the Brain Waves

For several centuries, from the seventeen to the early 20th century, it was often said that Britannia ruled the waves, referring to the strength and power of the British Navy. It was seldom challenged. Like the British Navy, before Google, Explorer, and Wikipedia were even imagined, for over 100 years there was the Encyclopedia Britannica. It was the trusted and reliable source for knowledge for millions of students and teachers around the world. If you needed to find out something on almost anything in the world, if you had access to the encyclopedia there was a better than 90%

chance you could find out something about the topic in one of its many volumes.

When I was teaching Biology at Roxborough High School in the fall of 1967, I was approached by an Encyclopedia Britannica salesman. He spieled out all the advantages of owning a set, including a multi-language dictionary, atlas, access to research papers for 10 years, and yearly updates. Being a student in a graduate program at the same time and getting married the following year, I thought this would be a great resource for myself, as well as our children in the future. Since the set was expensive, I purchased it on a payment plan.

The twenty plus deep red and gold trimmed volumes sat proudly on my bookshelf for many years. I used my set for many years as did my kids growing up in the seventies and eighties. In the early nineties, with the growth of computer technology companies like Microsoft, which were giving away encyclopedias like Encarta on disks with new computer purchases or for almost nothing, and with improved and faster access to the World Wide Web, search engines were born, and people were offering their volumes of the Encyclopedia Britannica online, with few takers.

My cherished set lasted into the early 21st century before it was dismissed from our bookcase. Only the multi-language dictionary and the atlas remain, even though the names and boundaries of the many countries found within its hallowed pages have changed.

Chapter 2: Tales from the Family Vault

This collection of stories provides some insight into the Zakroffs, where they came from, why they behave as they do, and the people and events that shaped my life.

The Progenitor, Zachariah Zakharov

Ever wonder where your family's immigrant ancestors came from? Before Ancestry.com asked you to spit in a bottle to learn about your past, and other genealogy websites like MyHeritage became popular, I had a cousin, David Snyder, who did an amazing job of gathering information about our family and assembling it into an easy-to-read format. It took him three years of research.

David's findings covered 8 generations of Zakharovs and Zakharov cousins going back to our common progenitor, Zachariah Zakharov (1785-1850 c.). The surname Zakharov corresponds to the Russian orthography. Various branches of the family adopted different spellings in the United States, like Zacheroff or Zackeroff. However, I always told my son, Dennis, an ice hockey goalie, he'd be better at the game if he used the original spelling.

The traceable origins of our family go back to the earliest known settlement of Jews in the town of Kraslava. Zachariah most likely came from a town in Latvia. Many in the Zakharov family were blacksmiths, a tradition which seems to have affected the professional choices of many in the Philadelphia and Chicago branches of the family who came to the United States between 1895 and 1906. My grandfather, Charles, was originally a blacksmith when he arrived in Philadelphia.

Today, the many descendants of Zachariah Zakharov are scattered throughout the United States and the world. Their varied occupations include accountants, artists, doctors, lawyers, and educators. To make David Snyder's effort more accessible to my family, including our children, grandchildren, and close relatives, my oldest son, Stephen, made pdfs of the entire work and put it into a Google folder allowing it to be easily examined using today's technology.

The Family Gene Pool

With all the scientific breakthroughs over the past twenty years or so, scientists have identified many different genes in the body. *Genes* play an important role in determining physical traits — how we look —and lots of other things about us. They carry information that makes us who we are and what we look like. Genes can determine if your hair is curly or straight, if you have long or short legs, even how we smile or laugh. Many of these things are passed from one generation to the next in a family by genes. And I know it's true.

My wife, Terry, has what I call a clean gene. I haven't seen it classified, but it's something I know she inherited from her mother, Natalie. Almost every day, my wife is sweeping the cork floor in the great room, cleaning a second bathroom used by my surfing college-age grandson, Stephen, who lives with us, and vacuums the rugs upstairs and downstairs. I think she can hear a piece of dirt fall on the floor or spot a speck of food dropping from the dinner table. She's on it in an instant and it's gone.

She also has what I call the religious gene. She goes to mass faithfully six times a week, donates to the church, delivers communion to home-bound seniors, and participates in bible study.

Now, when it comes to the Zakroffs, we inherited a completely different set of genes. When I talk with my sister, Betsy, about our family's gene pool, it's often about being short-tempered, impulsive, driven, as well as other things, such as the love of writing and gardening. These are things we have in common. Some of these traits we can see in our children and grandchildren. Hopefully, they only received the good ones.

Asbury Park Before Springsteen

Some places and experiences you never forget. When I was about six or seven years old in the early 1950's, our parents would take us on Sunday trips to Asbury Park, now famous for Bruce Springsteen. It was a long ride from Philly, but there was lots to see along the way as we crossed the Tacony-Palmyra Bridge into Jersey. The sights included acres and acres of farmland, pine forests, a lakeside park and water recreation area stacked with pleasure boats that I could never find again.

Once in Asbury Park, we would go on the amusements found on the boardwalk, like the Ferris wheel and bumper cars. We would even take paddleboat rides on the small lake nearby. I have a picture of that as proof. It was a fun outing we all enjoyed. When my mother passed in 1956 the trips stopped.

More than sixty years later I returned to Asbury Park on a business project. The company I was working for had offices in a high-rise building near what once was the amusement park. From their 7th floor windows I could see where I had once been including the paddleboat lake I remembered from my childhood.

Where is She?

As a youngster I knew very little about diseases except for chicken pox and scarlet fever, both of which I contracted at an early age. I knew my mother, Beatrice, was sick but what she had was kept from us. It was breast cancer. She had it for several years.

Back in the 1950's the most common treatment was a mastectomy. By the time she had the operation, the cancer had metastasized to different parts of her body. As it spread, she slowly lost her ability to speak and think. Every day after school, we would check on her in the front bedroom and in the evening kiss her goodnight. As the days and weeks went by, she hardly seemed to recognize us.

On the morning of June 13, 1956, things were different. When I got up and went to the bathroom to get ready for school, the door to the bedroom was open. I looked in and she was gone. I never saw her body and wasn't asked to go to her funeral. For many years I hoped and believed she was still alive and would come back to us. That never happened.

The Help

Though we didn't live in the South or reside in a mansion, as my mother became weaker from her cancer in the 1950's, my parents hired live-in housekeepers to keep our home clean and prepare the family meals. These women were all Afro-American and slept in the fourth bedroom upstairs.

One of the first housekeepers I remember was Miss Edna. She was a small, round black woman in her early 60's. Edna always had a smile on her face and never complained about the work. She stayed with us for a few years until the job became too much for her. She was assisted by a young black woman named Cilla, whose mother, Bertha, worked for neighbors across the driveway. Cilla was only in her teens at the time and completed tasks that Edna couldn't.

Shortly after our mother passed in 1956 my father, Louie, hired Ms. Beatrice, another black woman. She had the same name as our mother and picked up where Edna left off, cleaning the house, washing, and preparing our meals. She also stayed for several years.

As we grew older, we no longer required a sleep-in housekeeper. So, when Beatrice left, my father hired Dorothy Pitts. Dorothy would come in every morning, five days a week, clean the house, and cook dinner. On weekends we were on our own.

At the same time, we had a laundress come in once a week. Her name was Lucille. She was a big black woman and would iron clothes in the basement. However, she had a problem. She liked to take things from the house when people weren't looking and hide them under her clothes or in her big handbag. Dorothy had seen this happen and told my father about it. However, he let it slide. Apparently, he didn't want to look for another laundress.

When my brother and I left the nest in the late 1960's, Louie still had Dorothy coming in five-days a week to take care of the house and prepare his dinner.

Bathtub Serenades

Many romantic movies in the 1930's and 40's often featured a serenade. Nelson Eddy, a well-known performer at the time was famous for serenading Jeanette MacDonald either outside her window or in a canoe.

My father sang a lot also, both in the car to the radio and in the bathtub. He didn't have a great voice but was a man who worked hard at his true craft: buying and selling industrial equipment. He never stopped buying or selling up to and including his dying day at the age of 78. And, he never stopped singing. However, the words he sang differed by the situation. If it was a good day, you could hear him singing "The Yellow Rose of Texas," or, "She wore a yellow ribbon," while driving to a customer to close a potential sale.

However, we could easily tell when he had a rough day, like if he lost a sale or had an argument with his brother, Dave, at the office. On one of those days, after dinner he would take a hot bath in the upstairs bathroom next to his bedroom. You could hear the pipes shake as he rapidly turned the hot and cold faucets on and off to adjust the water temperature. Then the usual serenade would begin.

The words weren't repeatable, but Louie was letting off steam. Occasionally, to be smart, one of us would walk by the bathroom door, knock, and ask him if anything was wrong. We always received the same reply, "No. Nothing," and then the serenade would continue until his "song" finally ended as the water turned colder.

The No Show

My father wasn't happy that I was marrying out of my religion. It didn't matter that my sister, Betsy, had already done the deed several years earlier. On September 14th, 1968, our wedding day, I got up early and went to Joe's Barbershop on Cheltenham Avenue for an 8:00 am appointment and got my first professional shave and a haircut.

I then returned to my family home on Georgian Road and picked up my tuxedo. Within a few minutes, a good friend and member of the wedding party, Steve Parness, arrived in his little blue sports car and drove us to my bride's house on South 6th street where we dressed for the coming days' events.

By the time we got there, my brother, Rob, was already on the scene. As he was getting into his tux, he noticed the shirt was missing. Not to be alarmed, my father-in-law had a long sleeve white shirt that fit the bill.

The morning preparations went quickly. Before I knew it I was standing at the front of the church altar, waiting for the bride-to-be. As the ceremony began, I looked around the church. There were friends and relatives. However, someone was missing. My father wasn't there.

After the wedding ceremony, Terry's Uncle Paul drove us to the reception at the 4 Chefs caterers in the northeast. My in-laws had prepared a place for my father and his girlfriend, Lillian, but they were a "no show" for this event also.

Following the reception, my brother drove us to the airport for a short flight to Newark Airport, with a morning flight the next day to Jamaica where we spent a week on our honeymoon. Not sure who made the mistake, but that first night at the airport motel had twin beds. A great way to start a honeymoon.

Louie eventually showed up at our apartment, a no show no longer. I never asked him why he didn't come to the wedding. My father was who he was, and you never questioned his actions. A year later, when our son Stephen was born, he did show up for the christening party.

Working for the Man

Learning the ins and outs of a business from a family member can be tough. When I tried working for my father in the early 1970's, it was an experience I'll never forget. My dad wasn't "old school." He was from the first school. In his office on North 3rd street in Philadelphia, he would hand me books with illustrations of machine tools. They weren't instruction manuals; they were just pictures of machines. Louie was partner with his next younger brother, Dave. They were together for more than 30 years.

When he would send me out to look at machine tools he was considering bidding on at auction or buying, I was told to measure the size of the chucks on the metal working lathes and write down the serial number on each tool. I also needed to check for cracks and wear and see what spare parts or special equipment were included as part of the sale. In addition, I often took a polaroid shot of the machine for him to examine.

When he had a machine in his warehouse on Germantown Avenue that a customer was interested in, he'd have me take a photograph of it. Many times, this required climbing on or over other machines stacked on top of each other. It was almost like mountain climbing but without any safety lines to grab on to. I also had to watch out for Nipper, the foreman's dog who relished going after my ankles while I was in the shop. Eddie, the shop foreman, had been with my father and uncle since the end of World War II and knew everything about metalworking machines and how to repair them.

One thing I'll always remember after my first experience checking out a machine for Louie, was the question, "How far was it from the door or loading dock and would the seller load it?" That was something he never told me about in advance; something he knew but kept in his head. Answering that question was important in figuring the price to offer the seller; what was it going to cost to move the piece to the door and load it on a truck?

Lou and Dave would buy and sell machines up and down the east coast. When they came across a DC motor, they would take it apart for the copper and sell it to a scrap dealer for cash. They often bought machines by weight, so if they didn't sell they could get their money back in scrap. They would take the motors off these machines and sell them individually. From time to time somebody needed a motor or something and my father had them, plenty of them. I recall him selling 100 tons of motors to a company from South America for three cents a pound. That was a lot of motors and it added up to a lot of cents.

After a year of the machinery business, I just couldn't see myself doing it for the rest of my life. Though there was money to be made, this wasn't how I wanted to make it. So, when a training job with Boeing Vertol appeared I left.

Dining with Louie

My father loved to go to the Bluebell Inn in Montgomery County, PA for dinner on Saturday night with his on-off-again lady friend, Lillian Mann. On a weekend my sister and brother were in the Philly area, he invited my wife and I to join them for dinner at the Inn. It was about an hour and twenty-minute ride from where we lived in Cinnaminson, NJ to the restaurant.

We left our home about 3:30 for an early dinner with the family. We arrived at the Inn at about 4:45. My father, sister and brother were there waiting for us. We were seated promptly, and all had dinner. I remember having prime rib, one of my favorite meals. However, before you could say "Jack Robinson," my father had finished his meal, usually chicken, and was ready to leave. Forget about dessert or sitting and chatting. That was not his cup of tea.

When it was time to pay the bill and leave a tip, my father picked up the tab, and then left a two-dollar tip for the entire dinner had by seven people, which at the time was at least $140.00 dollars. I saw the waitress signal the manager with two fingers. They knew my father, as he was a regular, and his tight tipping habits. I alerted my siblings to the signs. We looked at each other, shook our heads, and quickly added additional funds to make it a reasonable gratuity. Upon exiting the Inn, with our meals not yet reaching our stomachs, we made the trip back to Cinnaminson in 45 minutes. The whole elapsed time, to the restaurant, dinner, and the return was less than three hours.

Where's Louie?

My father never really took care of himself in his later years. He ate the wrong things and never listened to his doctors. The only thing he thought about was making a buck, right up until his dying day. We often kidded that his suit would go into work without him. A few days before he passed, Louie was in the hospital for diabetes and a related kidney problem.

He had collapsed a few days before outside his home and a neighbor called the police who took him to Germantown hospital. Two days later, he checked himself out. He then had someone drive him up towards Allentown to look at a piece of machinery he was interested in buying.

I would check on my father at least once a week with a phone call as my sister and brother lived out of the area. The day after leaving the hospital, I couldn't reach him by phone, either at his office at Germantown and Berks Streets, or at his home. His secretary, Roberta, said she didn't know where he was and hadn't heard from him.

I called my father-in-law, Marty, and asked him if he would take a ride with me to Louie's home in West Oak Lane, as I didn't really want to go into that neighborhood alone. He agreed and I picked him up in South Philadelphia, and we went to my father's house together.

When we arrived, I saw my father's car parked on the street and thought he could be home. I went up the concrete steps and rang the doorbell several times. There was no answer. I no longer had a key to the house, as Louie had lost his and I had given him mine.

My next thought was that maybe someone had driven him to look at the machine and he had left his car home. So, we left. I then drove my father-in-law back to South Philly and went home. I figured I'd try and call Louie later.

As it became later in the afternoon, I tried calling both his office and home again, with no success. As evening approached, I made the decision to go back to his house and face the possibility that he had passed. My wife and I drove back to Philly and parked near his car, which had not moved since our earlier visit. I rang the doorbell again and he didn't answer. I then walked around to the back of the house and up to the rear steps to the porch and banged on the door. Still no answer.

The back door had four small windows. I then broke the window closest to the lock and let myself in. I called to my father, but there was no answer. I then walked through the home in search of him. He wasn't downstairs.

I then made my way up the steps to the second floor. It was then that I saw him. He was stretched out on the bed in the bedroom at the top of the stairs. He was gone. He had his clothes on and was just lying there in his grey suit. The TV was on, but it was just buzzing with a fuzzy screen. It was one time his suit couldn't go to work without him.

Are You Really Jewish?

As noted in my first book, and well documented in a written camp counselor report from Bob White Day Camp dated August 1950, I have interesting habits when it comes to food. I know what I like and what I don't. Seldom do I try new things. That's me. I can put something up to my nose, smell it, and almost immediately tell if it will agree with me or not. If I take a chance and make a mistake, my stomach will definitely tell me a short time later.

This boils down to a lot of ethnic treats often served at affairs like weddings and bat or bar mitzvahs, especially typically Jewish ones. I can easily gobble down a host of pigs in the blanket or chicken strips. Almost anything else the stomach says, "No! No!"

One Saturday I was at the bat mitzvah of my cousin Ellis's daughter. At the affair following the service, waiters were bringing different appetizers around to the tables of guests. My wife, Terry, and I were seated with several other first cousins and their spouses. When the waiter approached and asked me what I wanted from the tray, I said, "I'll pass." From what I could see, there was nothing on the tray I or my stomach wanted. Stanley, the husband of my cousin, Barbara, remarked, "Are you really Jewish?" I looked down below my waist and loosened my belt to check. Then, I looked up, smiled, and replied, "Yes, I am!"

Financing a College Education

In the hit Broadway Show, Evita, there's a song mentioning how to pay for a college education in Argentina by writing your name and your wish on a card, and if Evita selected it, she'd pay for your schooling. Problem is, this isn't Argentina and she's long gone.

My siblings and I were very lucky. Our parents weren't rich but put away money every month towards our college tuition. Though I didn't agree much with my father on anything, this was something I greatly appreciated. I had no college loan debt upon graduation, plus there was a little left over to start my life in the real world.

Following my father's lead, I began saving for my children's college tuition right after they were born. It wasn't a lot to start, but it grew. No matter the financial situation, we put away $10.00 a week towards each child's college fund. It was our routine. Slowly each account grew. When it became several hundred dollars or $1000, we'd invest in certificates or bank bonds. At one time, some were paying 9.5%.

When our first child, Stephen, was ready for college he won a full scholarship to St. Joseph's University. The money we had saved paid for his room and board, plus his masters. Our second son, Dennis, went to St. Bonaventure in Olean, New York for two years. He had thoughts of becoming a professional hockey goalie, but that wasn't in the cards. He graduated from Rutgers with a degree in Finance and Accounting, again with no college debt.

Our third child, Laura, went to the Rhode Island School of Design (RISD), one of the top art schools in the country on a partial scholarship. As we were saving for her education, the rules and interest rates were changing. The best deal at the time was investing in U.S. Savings Bonds and the interest was tax deductible. We took advantage of it.

In her case, we took out college loans as the school was very expensive, plus there were monthly costs for art supplies. However, the loans weren't payable until graduation. When Laura graduated, we were able to pay off the loans with the interest from the bonds. She too started life free of college loans.

As a middle-class guy who planned for his kids' educations, I get a little riled up when I see discussions about canceling all student loan debt. On one hand, I can see if families were given ridiculous interest rates that just ballooned their loan payback. That I can understand. However, if you just let your child pick a college that was out of your price range, or did no preplanning, spent all you had on luxuries like boats or second homes, or the child just quit, that upsets me. Few employers, except maybe high-end law firms or hospitals really care about where you went to school. They just want to know you can do the job they hired you for.

Cover Letters and Kids

I've had a great deal of experience writing job cover letters for myself and my children. When I was downsized from the Boeing Company in 1970, I created a one-piece visual cover letter and resume that could be made into a hat. The page included the design of a baseball cap, and on the sides were the talents I offered: Writer, Photographer, and Producer. The center of the hat-like letter contained my qualifications and experience. The idea was to stand out from others applying for the same position. I think it's a lot tougher today to stand out. So many job applications are submitted online and run through an algorithm before the person doing the hiring ever reads it.

When it comes to cover letters and our three children, Stephen, Dennis, and Laura, two write with quill pens and one writes with a brick. When my oldest son, Stephen, was applying for a position in funding and development at a well-known private school in the Moorestown area, he asked me to review his cover letter before sending it. One of the things he mentioned in his letter struck me funny. He told the school that he lived only a few minutes away. I said, "That's nice, but I don't think mentioning that will help you get the job. The school is more interested in your experience and what you can do for them." Steve did get the job and has been there for over 20 years. A rarity today. He hasn't had to write a job cover letter in years, just ones asking for donations, which can be a lot harder.

Honorable #2 son, Dennis, is a different story. He is more of a finance and accounting person than a writer. He's great with numbers and gathering facts but writing an effective cover letter was never his forte. Having written many cover letters over 50 years for proposals and projects, I've always been happy to help. What are parents for!

Depending upon the position he was applying for, I would often research an appropriate quotation to open the letter. It was different, often caught the prospective employer's attention, and a lot better than, "Dear sir, my name is ... and I am interested in applying for the position of..."

I fondly remember when he was applying for a dual position as Athletic Director and Business Manager for a local school district. To open the letter, we used a well-known quote from baseball great Yogi Berra and adapted it to the situation. "Baseball is 90 percent mental. The other half is physical." It was sports related, dealt with handling two jobs, and added a little humor to his introduction.

For another cover letter we opened with a quote from Albert Einstein: "We cannot solve our problems with the same thinking we used when we created them." And then tied it to the job being applied for and the qualities needed by the applicant... In today's ever evolving educational landscape, a school district needs a forward-thinking leader with knowledge and experience, as well as innovative ideas to overcome challenges as they arise.

With a little practice and encouragement, Dennis got the hang of it and eventually did his own research for quotes that were relevant to the jobs he was applying for.

When it comes to our youngest child, Laura, she didn't really need much assistance in writing cover letters because, unlike her brothers, she is in business for herself. Laura has an amazing grasp of the English language, is not afraid to speak her mind, and lets her many books and artwork do the talking for her. Check out her many publications on Amazon, under Laura Tempest Zakroff.

Gone, Baby, Gone

Just after my oldest son, Stephen, received his driver's license he went to the Cherry Hill Mall on a Friday night with Albert, a friend from school who lived up the street from us. My son is usually a pretty intelligent young man. He won a full scholarship, was in the top 10 of his high school graduating class, and a member of the National Honor Society. You couldn't do much better than that.

On one particular Friday evening he was driving our 1984 red, Ford Tempo, a luxury car by no means. It was the vehicle I had won at the local church carnival two years earlier. For about two hours, he and his friend, Albert, cruised the mall checking out clothes, food, and girls. It was the thing to do for many high school kids on a Friday night.

Before they knew it, the mall was preparing to close for the night. As the pair hurried out the exit, they noticed the car was gone. They looked all around but couldn't find it. Who'd want to steal a Ford Tempo? In a panic, Stephen called home to tell us his predicament. We said to call the police and check with mall security. We also told him, we'd come and pick the boys up.

Just as we were preparing to leave for the mall, we received another call from Stephen. They had found the car. No, it wasn't stolen. They had just gone out the wrong exit.

Chapter 3: South Jersey Living

For the initial 23 years of our married lives, my wife, Terry, and I resided in South Jersey. First in Marlton, NJ, then in Cinnaminson, just north of the Tacony-Palmyra Bridge. It was here that we raised our kids and made many life-long friends. This chapter retells many of our most memorable experiences.

Our First Place

My wife, Terry, and I were married in September of 1968. Since she was working in Philadelphia for Penn Mutual Insurance and I had a job with Ocean County College, we decided to find an apartment in South Jersey that would be an easy commute for her and a straight shot for me to Ocean County College outside of Toms River.

After checking out several apartment complexes in the Cherry Hill and the surrounding area, we settled on The Allison Apartments just off Route 70 in Marlton, New Jersey. They were constructing a new section of garden apartments that were supposed to be finished by the time we got married. Based on the plans shown to us at the rental office we selected a one-bedroom, first-floor corner. The rent was going to be $135 per month. At the time, that was a fair amount for a newlywed couple to handle.

As it turned out, there were construction delays which pushed back the occupancy date by several weeks. After our honeymoon in Jamaica, we ended up spending two weeks with my in-laws in South Philly, waiting for the apartment to be finished.

Finally, the apartment was granted a certificate of occupancy and we had our furniture delivered. It was a beautiful place with hardwood floors and some wood paneling. There were also sliding glass doors to a small patio where we placed a charcoal-burning hibachi to cook hamburgers and hot dogs.

The apartments had a central storage building near us. Each apartment had a caged-in space with a place for a lock. Being naïve newlyweds, we placed our snow tires in the space without covering them. Of course, when winter came and we went to get them, they were gone. Someone had cut the wire caging and taken the tires. A lesson learned.

For our first Christmas we decided to get a flocked tree which we purchased on Delaware Avenue in Philly. It was a beautiful tree, but the only flocked one we ever bought. Lesson Two. For as long as we had our Tempest, the car we brought it home in, there was always flocking in the trunk.

In addition to having a beautiful garden apartment, there was also a swimming pool on the grounds, which was great in the summer. Especially, when Terry was pregnant with our first child.

We lived at the Allison Apartments for a little less than two years. Then we purchased our first house in Cinnaminson, NJ. Our movers were Terry's father, Marty, and her Uncle Paul, a milkman, who worked for Sealtest. They had moving down to an exact science and carefully brought all our furniture and belongings to Cinnaminson without a scratch.

Christine, the Cursed Tempest

It you like horror movies you've probably watched the 1983 movie called "Christine." That movie was about a scary, 1958 Plymouth Fury. Apparently other cars can carry a curse also. Just before we got married in 1968, I bought a gold-colored, four-door Pontiac Tempest. It was a beautiful car. However, it was hit on the passenger's side door in the exact same spot three times. If that's not cursed, I don't know what else it could be.

The first time the curse appeared was when my wife was driving it to work in Philadelphia from our apartment in Marlton. It was only a short drive, one that she made on a daily basis, but on this day, a driver swerved into her and crunched the door. Thank goodness she wasn't hurt, just shaken up.

Not long after that we had the door repaired. A few days later we were celebrating our anniversary at the Farm Restaurant, near Cherry Hill, and going around the famous Ellisburg Circle. When all of a sudden two great danes appeared out of nowhere, one chasing the other. They sideswiped the car. Guess where? The passenger's side door. The dogs ran off and again, no one was injured.

Several months later, I went to a small food market on Church Road, just down the road from where we lived in Marlton, New Jersey. When I started to leave the store, I couldn't believe my eyes. An old pickup truck had lost its brakes and rolled right into the newly repaired door.

The third time was the straw that broke the Tempest's back. Within a few weeks of repairing the door for the third and final time, we traded it in and tried our luck with a Buick LeSabre.

Crossing the Delaware

Unlike George Washington who crossed the Delaware to attack the British in Trenton on Christmas Eve, I crossed that river on a daily basis to get to work for several months. Though I didn't have a long boat, I did have a ferry.

After leaving a very unhappy work experience at Ocean County College, in Toms River, NJ, my job was as an instructional associate with The Service Project Area Research Center (SPARC) in West Chester, PA. It was a forerunner to the Pennsylvania Intermediate Units for Chester and Delaware Counties.

At the time we were still living at the Allison Apartments. This new job required me to travel to West Chester every day. The best way to get to West Chester from Marlton, NJ was to take Route 295 South to Route 322 and take the Chester-Bridgeport Ferry across the Delaware River. (There was no Commodore Barry Bridge at the time.) Once I got off the ferry, I followed Route 322 to Route 1 South and then took 202 into West Chester where SPRAC's offices were located. Then, at the end of the day, I would retrace my steps back to Marlton, NJ.

The ferry was always an interesting ride especially on Friday nights. The ferry could only accommodate so many cars and trucks on a crossing. More than once truckers would get into an argument on the ferry and bring everything to a standstill. On those nights I never knew how long it would take to get home. Hopefully it would be before Christmas, or when the British would retake Trenton.

Teaching what you know best

When we first moved to Cinnaminson in 1970, I was looking for ways to supplement my income. After seeing an adult education course catalog offered by the school district, I came up with an idea. It was to teach an evening class at the local high school on a subject that was close to my heart and that I had a fair amount of successful experience with: Magazine Article Writing. In college my journalism teachers always said, "Write about what you know." I did and was able to generate income from it. Here my plan was to teach what I knew best and earn additional revenue using that experience.

In college, graduate school, and afterwards I had published articles in *The Philadelphia Inquirer Sunday Magazine*, *Highlights for Children*, *Design*, (a publication for art teachers), as well as numerous other publications. I had also taught students in junior high how to write and sell articles as a means for getting them to know the ins and outs of the English language and what you could do with that knowledge and ability.

Based on the college course I had taken several years earlier at Temple, I developed a topic outline spread over eight weeks and presented it to the directors of the adult education programs at both Cinnaminson High School, and Moorestown High School, the neighboring township. I figured that if one district wasn't interested maybe another one would. To my surprise, both programs were interested in offering the course during the next semester. If enough people signed up for the class, a minimum of ten, the class would be a go.

As it turned out, more than enough people in both districts signed up and I was teaching it one night a week at each high school. Each class was composed of a wide range of people who ranged in age from their 20's to their 60's. They all had different ideas for articles. Week by week we went through the process of identifying and defining topics and possible magazines interested in them, writing query letters, and developing and rewriting their pieces. In the end, several students did get their articles published, while others received rejection letters, something many writers including me have received from time to time. The secret is to keep writing – if that's your passion.

Every Family Needs a Pet

My wife always had dogs as pets at her family home in South Philadelphia. Her first was, Snooky, a German Shepard that didn't make it in through police K-9 training due to a hip displacement problem. When we were dating her family had two dogs that they kept in the backyard: Pirate, a friendly beagle, and Rinnie, a water spaniel gifted to the family by her Aunt Millie.

When we got married pets were not allowed at our apartment in Marlton, NJ. However, that didn't stop us from thinking about getting one. We looked at a white Samoyed one weekend. It was tough to say no, especially when the pet shop puts you in a corral with it.

In the end, we settled on a rabbit we saw in the window of a pet shop in Cherry Hill. We named it Fifi. This cuddly rabbit was brown and white and easy to housebreak. It learned to do its business on a tray of newspaper in the kitchen and he slept on a rug in our bedroom at night. During the day, while we were at work, he would sit by the sliding glass doors at the back of the apartment and sun himself. When we were home, we would occasionally take it for a walk on a leash.

Several months later, when our first son, Stephen, was born. He developed a rash. The pediatrician thought he might be allergic to fur, like that of the rabbit. One of them had to go. The son or the rabbit. Reluctantly we chose the son over the rabbit and donated the bunny to a shelter. I still wonder whether or not we made the right choice.

A year later we moved from the apartment to a house in Cinnaminson, NJ. Shortly thereafter, our second child, Dennis, was born. As our kids were getting older, we considered getting a dog for a pet and to give the boys some responsibility. One Sunday we saw an advertisement in the Philadelphia Inquirer for Husky pups for sale. The seller was located in South Jersey. We called, made an appointment, and took a ride to their home in Washington Township.

They had several pups, both male and female. Our eyes went to one particularly playful husky who was gray and white in color. He pranced around the owner's yard as if giving an audition and gave a winning performance. Before much time passed, we had settled on a price and were on the way home with the little rascal we named Beowolf.

We kept Beowolf for about eight years. He was really an outside dog, so we built a run for him in our backyard using a heavy metal hoist cable I got from my father's warehouse. We also constructed a doghouse for him. Beowolf loved to go up and down the run. In fact, one day he became unhooked from the run but kept running up and down it until we noticed. When we had a party in the backyard Beowolf would often help us clean up by chewing any cigarette butts and licking the last drop from any beer cans. Then he would come up and try and give us a kiss.

Beowolf would very seldom bark, but he had a stare that could send shivers up your spine. My friend Neal would hesitate to come through our breezeway if Beowolf was there, because the dog would give him that stare.

With the birth of our daughter, Laura, seven years later, Beowolf changed. He was no longer the third child in our family and started to show aggressive tendencies. He began growling, gritting his teeth, and running away. For everyone's safety we sadly took him to a local shelter in the hopes that he would find a new home.

As my daughter, Laura, got older she wanted a pet to call her own. As it happened, one day we had a major rainstorm followed by flooding from a nearby creek off of New Albany Road. Looking outside, coming down the street was a large box turtle. It became her pet. We purchased a terrarium for it to live in and fed it ground beef and strawberries.

It was interesting to see the creature put the ground beef in its mouth and chomp away. When her turtle phase passed, we released the critter back into the creek where it may still be alive today. Turtles do have a long lifespan.

Several years later, at Christmas time, my daughter asked for a dog. She wanted a beagle. Searching through the

Sunday papers we saw an ad for beagle pups and decided to check it out on a weekend afternoon. The seller was located near Vineland, NJ, about an hour's ride from our home in Cinnaminson. When we arrived at this rural site, the farm was loaded with pups. My daughter picked a male out of the litter, which she named Dickens. As it turned out, these beagles were bred for hunting rather than just pets. Dickens defied housebreaking crate training. Within a few months, he had a new owner.

With the departure of Dickens from our family, we were pet-less, but for only a short time. As it turned out, one of the teachers where my wife taught had a mini-lop rabbit who had just delivered a litter and she was looking for families interested in adopting the bunnies. Before you could say, "Jack Robinson," a six-week-old male rabbit, which my wife named Puck, like hockey puck, joined our family.

Puck looked like a wild rabbit you see running around the forest but with floppy ears. He was very smart and easy to house break. He learned to do his business on newspaper, enjoyed stretching out on the fireplace hearth, and allowed us to hold him like a baby without scratching. Puck was even good at being a stud as he fathered several litters with a female mini-lop from the high school where our kids went to high school. I remember even giving the two rabbits carrots after one mating session. It reminded me of scenes on television of couples smoking cigarettes after having had sex.

Puck went with us everywhere. During summers at the shore, he would run up and down the hallway banging into doors as he explored each room. When we moved to South Carolina in 1993, Puck went with us. We had to get special permission to fly, but he survived the flight. In South Carolina I built a raised hutch for Puck to live in near the house. That turned out to be an error.

One weekend while my wife and I were in Atlanta, we received a tearful call from our daughter, Laura. Apparently, a neighbor's large hunting dog got loose and spooked Puck, causing him to break his back. Rabbits have very fragile nervous systems. Puck was just laying there unable to move. There was nothing the vet could do for him. The humane thing to do was to put him down.

In an attempt to quell our sorrow, we sought a replacement for Puck. We found another mini-lop, which we named Spooky. He was black and white in color but had been raised in a different environment than Puck. He wasn't friendly or cuddly and was difficult to housebreak. As a result, he spent a great deal of time in the hutch.

However, the hutch was his undoing and led to his untimely demise. This time the neighbor's dogs knocked down the hutch from its moorings and made a meal of Spooky. All we found were a few pieces of black and white fur. That was a sign to us that we really weren't wanted in the South and before long put the house up for sale. We also put a pause on pets as we didn't know what the future would hold for us.

The Invisible Umpire

Watching an umpire call balls and strikes in a professional baseball game can be frustrating. How many times in a game you're watching on television or at the stadium do you wonder what the heck he was seeing or if he was paying attention at all. It's often been said in many sports that an umpire or referee has called a good game if he or she is invisible when it comes to the final results of the event.

However, you really don't know the pain and anxiety an umpire goes through in trying to do a good job, unless you've tried it yourself. I had the luxury, or you could say the misfortune of going through that experience myself. And it ain't easy.

When we first moved to Cinnaminson my next-door neighbor, Russ Waite, was in charge of scheduling referees for little league baseball games in town. One week he was running short of volunteers for this wonderful, non-paying opportunity. Wanting to get involved in township sports, even though my own kids were too young to participate, I offered to help out. How difficult could it be? I had refereed touch football and soccer games in college, and I thought I knew baseball pretty well, having played it for many years.

My initial assignment was to umpire an early evening game being played by two 11-year-old teams at a field off of Taylor's Lane. My equipment included a counter for balls and strikes, score card, a mask, a chest protector, and a small broom to clean home plate. What I really needed was a pair of earmuffs and a Valium. After receiving the line ups from each parent manager, I said, "Play ball" and the game began.

I crotched down behind the catcher, like they do in professional games, and called balls and strikes as I saw them. It didn't take long before the managers on both teams were questioning my calls and where I saw the strike zone. The way the managers were chirping at me you would have thought it was Billy Martin and Tony LaRussa playing the seventh game of the world series.

I guess I was lucky that one of them didn't come over and kick dirt on my shoes. If there was a close play at the plate, I called it as I saw it. I couldn't call New York for a replay. If there was a play at first or third, I called it as I saw it since there was only one ump, and that was me. No matter what a manager said, I didn't need glasses.

By the time the game reached the bottom of the seventh inning, the normal length of these little-league events, I was tired, frustrated, and covered with dust. And that was just on the outside. After the last out, I walked off the field, got into my car and drove home.

The next day, I went to the doctor for some physical therapy as I had a pain in the neck that stayed around for several days. When I talked to my neighbor, Russ, about the game, he said the managers weren't happy with my umpiring, but they said I didn't favor either team. After that experience I decided to become really invisible and never volunteer for that duty again.

The Commish

When my first son, Stephen, reached the age of seven he became eligible to play in the different sports programs offered by Cinnaminson township. The programs included basketball, baseball, and soccer. The first sport I signed him up for was soccer. Cinnaminson was a hotbed for soccer activity and fielded in-town and travel teams. The in-town program was also looking for coaches.

The cost for playing soccer in town was $10.00 per child. For the ten bucks your child received a pair of socks and a team jersey. Parents were asked to participate in some way like coaching, refereeing, or running the lines when balls went out of bounds during games. Having played the game in high school, and intramural programs in college, I felt qualified to coach my son and other boys his age.

Also, since I worked from home, I had the luxury of being able to run practice sessions in the late afternoons after school as practice times and fields were at a premium. I held two practices a week, weather permitting, usually on Tuesday and Thursday during the season. Each session was about an hour long. During each practice we worked on the basics of dribbling, passing, and shooting, as well as positioning, goaltending and penalty shots.

Games were played on Saturdays at Wood Park, often before crowds of cheering parents and relatives. At half-time parents provided oranges and water for the team on a rotating basis. My assistant coach that first year was Walt Morton who lived on the other side of town. Walt worked for New Jersey Bell Telephone. I remember it well as one day he called me from the top of the Walt Whitman bridge while doing a repair job for the telephone company. My teams usually did well. In fact, one year we went undefeated and won the championship.

Many of the players on my first team went on to play on the travel teams, including my son Stephen, Kevin Dirzik, Brad Bayard, and Walt's son, Doug.

During my second year of coaching, I was asked by the current soccer commissioner, Jim Russell, a tech specialist, if I would be interested in becoming the next commissioner as he was moving out of Cinnaminson. I discussed it with my wife and accepted. Of course, I didn't know what I was getting into. Besides the politics of getting along with the commissioners of the other sports, there was constant friction between the in-town soccer program and the travel teams.

The "fun" began with signing up for the program. It was like pulling teeth to get parents to help with the signups. On one Saturday morning, we had signups for the program. Parents signed up their kids and paid the $10.00 registration fee, they also indicated their participation level: coach, assistant coach, or linesman. They were also given a time for player tryouts to gauge the skill level of each player in order to have a draft and balance the teams so no one team was a powerhouse.

During the tryouts, several experienced coaches rated the kids on their abilities to kick, trap, dribble, pass and shoot. The scores were placed on 3 x 5 cards and assembled in descending order from highest to lowest.

At the player draft, each team was given a number which was placed in a hat. Coaches drew numbers and selected players in that order, based on the ratings on the cards.

High school soccer players were recruited to referee the games which were played on Saturdays and also Sunday afternoons. The commissioner's job included making a schedule for the games, setting practice times and assigning fields for each team.

This was all for the in-town teams. The travel teams were another story. They wanted the best fields and extra practice times, even on Sunday mornings which was a "No-No!" in Cinnaminson. Sunday morning was for church. You would think these guys were preparing for "The World Cup."

On top of all the behind-the-scenes work, I took a team myself, coaching my younger son, Dennis, who wanted to be a goalie.

After a year as commissioner, I had had enough of the politics and stress. It wasn't like I was getting paid for this "fun." I kept coaching as long as I had a child in the program, including my daughter, Laura, who at the time was more interested in chasing butterflies on the field than playing, but let the group of coaches select their next commissioner.

Good Fences Make Good Neighbors

The proverb "Good fences make good neighbors," is attributed to the American poet Robert Frost, and I believe it to be true. When you move into a neighborhood, you seldom know who your next-door neighbors will be or what they are capable of. When we first moved into Cinnaminson, NJ, the Lutz family, Steve and Carole, and their two girls, lived on one side. On the other side was the Waite family, Russ and Carole and their four boys. The backyards of the three properties were bordered by a three-foot split-rail fence. All three families got along great. There were pool parties, dinners, and even cross-yard tomato fights.

After a few years the Lutz's got divorced and put their house up for sale. It was a nice 3-bedroom colonial with a wide range of amenities. The house wasn't on the market long when it was purchased by a family we called "The Walnuts." When we first met them, the wife was in a body cast due to an accident. The husband, Stanley, seemed like a nice guy, even though he worked for the IRS. They had three children. The eldest was a daughter, Debra, and there were two sons, Michael and Ronald.

Over the next few years we lived in relative peace with them. It was nothing like when the Lutz family lived next door. Stanley's wife made a point of letting us know that almost everything they had was due to her ability to sue.

Now, in our backyard, closest to their property was a doghouse I had constructed for our pet husky, Beowolf, and a small garden where I planted vegetables. Along the back of the properties was that split rail fence that went along the property line that separated us from the farm behind.

Though we didn't have much contact with them, the Walnut's son, Michael, had a reputation around the neighborhood and at school as a troublemaker and a bully.

The other kids in the area hated him. In fact, one day they cornered him and tied him to a pole.

On one late spring evening, we were in our backyard playing with our children, when Michael got up on the fence and started yelling. I told him to get down and go away and thought nothing of it.

About an hour later, when we were giving our kids a bath, the phone rang. It was a neighbor's son across the street, Ron Tedeschi. He said there was a police officer at our door.

I greeted the officer at the door. Apparently, he had come to arrest me. Mrs. Walnut had accused me of hitting her darling son with a hammer and wanted me taken away in handcuffs. I explained to the officer that nothing of the kind had taken place. However, a complaint had been filed and I would have to go to court to defend myself.

I immediately called my brother, Rob, a practicing lawyer in Washington, D.C., Maryland, and Virginia for advice. He told me to take pictures to document the scene. He also petitioned the local court "as a friend" to defend me. It was granted.

The court date was to be a few weeks later. In the meantime, I took polaroid pictures of the area of the supposed incident and a hammer I kept in the garage: the alleged weapon. At the same time the orchestrator of the crime was telling everyone in the neighborhood that they were going to get our car and our pool.

On the day of the court appearance, I picked up my brother at the 30th Street train station in Philly. On the way to our home we discussed the strategy. My brother told me to remain calm and let him do all the talking. If I was asked questions by the township prosecutor, I was to keep my answers short and to the point. At the local courthouse many friends and neighbors showed up to support me.

When my case came up, my brother set the scene with the pictures I had taken and interrogated the Walnuts about the incident. No one had seen me strike Michael, as he and his mother claimed. They didn't even take him to the hospital after the alleged incident to document any injuries. The Walnuts' daughter, Debra, told the truth about what had supposedly happened. As a result of her testimony the case was dismissed.

My brother told us that based on their false claims we could sue them, but we decided against it. The next day, the gas tank of my wife's station wagon parked in front of our house was stuffed with stones and dirt. Guess who? However, we couldn't prove it or try to.

So we didn't have to look at these people again, we had a six-foot wooden privacy fence erected on our side of the property line. On the outside, facing the Walnuts' property, we posted "No Trespassing" signs every four feet.

Within a year they moved to another part of town.

The Cinnaminson Sheriff

My image of a peace officer or marshal harkens back to TV westerns like Gunsmoke's Matt Dillon, Wyatt Earp, or Walker, Texas Ranger. When we lived in Cinnaminson, NJ, I would go to the local coffee shop at around 8:00 am before going to the Post Office to pick up my business mail. It wasn't posted until around 8:30. One of the regulars at the coffee shop was Tom Adams, the local chief of police. At the time, Chief Adams was a tall thin, balding man in his mid to late fifties. He really didn't fit my image of a chief of police. In fact, I never saw him in uniform, and he drove around town in a small red Ford pickup.

However, at the coffee shop, I noticed he would always sit with his back to the wall. I'm sure it was a habit borne of years of police work. Like a sheriff or marshal in a B western, no one could get behind the Chief in any situation. What I remember most about Chief Adams, was a comment he made after I had won a car at the yearly catholic church carnival. He remarked, "What do they do with the Protestant tickets, put them in the trash?"

Blueberry Heaven

Several years ago on a warm summer afternoon, I was returning to my home in Cinnaminson, NJ, from a client meeting in Central New Jersey. As I traveled south on Route 9 through Middlesex County, I chanced upon a family-owned farm stand called Wemrock Farms. Quite often, if I see an interesting spot on my travels I stop and examine the offerings. You never know what treats you may find. I pulled off the highway and into their parking lot and went to see what they had.

They had many of the standard fruits and vegetables to offer, like corn and tomatoes. However, what caught my eye were these beautiful blueberry muffins. They were golden yellow in color, had visible berries throughout, and a light sugary coating. I bought a half-dozen and sampled one on my way home. It was out of this world. Wemrock Farms made my list of places to stop. Whenever I'm up in that neck of the woods, Wemrock Farms is on my itinerary. Hopefully, they still have some muffins when I get there.

No Way Out

We lived in Cinnaminson for 23 years and had a great many friends there. One family we were close with was Pat and Rich Millilo. Pat was a homemaker and Rich worked in clothing procurement for the government. They had four kids: three boys, Richie, Stephen and David, and a girl, Donna. My wife and Pat were good friends and even had a small craft business at one time called The Wild Strawberry.

One year, on a President's Day weekend, we decided to take our families on an educational road trip to New York to visit the United Nations building and the Statue of Liberty. Early that Monday morning we all loaded into my wife's Ford Country Squire wagon and headed up the New Jersey Turnpike towards the Big Apple.

Since it was a holiday, traffic was relatively light and we made good time reaching the Lincoln Tunnel. As we went through the tunnel, my wife closed her eyes and held her breath. She hated tunnels. Once safely through the tunnel, we headed down towards the UN building. As we approached our initial destination, we started looking for a parking garage or lot. We circled the building several times, but all the lots we saw were closed or full.

As we widened our search, Rich saw a multi-level parking garage with the door open. Figuring our luck had changed, we drove in and down several levels until we found a parking spot. All the way down we never saw another person or an attendant and thought nothing of it at the time. Once parked, we then walked up several flights of steps and exited to the street.

By now it was early afternoon, and we had a choice to make. We could either go to the UN or visit Lady Liberty. We couldn't do both as originally planned. A vote by the adults favored "The Statue of Liberty," so off we went to the waterfront a few blocks away to catch a boat ride to "The Lady."

We didn't have to wait long, paid the fare for our troupe, and accomplished at least one of our goals for the day. We returned to the dock about two hours later and walked back to the parking garage. We then retraced our steps down to the level the car was on, loaded our families and drove back up towards the entrance. Not sure how much the cost of the parking was going to be, we all pulled several dollars out of our wallets. However, when we reached the garage door, it was down. There was no person around. No button to open the door. There was nobody. We were stuck.

Rich and I got out of the car and searched for an attendant. We walked down a level and finally found a service phone. We tried it, but no one answered. I guess the attendant was off for the holiday. Here we were locked in a parking garage in New York City with a car full of kids, but we couldn't get out.

We began to weigh our options for escape. There weren't many. After much discussion and growing frustration, we decided to ram the garage door and worry about the damages later. As we drove the car towards the door, it seemed to magically open, like someone had spoken the magic words, "open sesame."

As it turned out, this was a private garage, not a public one, and a renter was driving in just as we were preparing to escape. As harrowing as it was at the time, we all had a good laugh about the adventure afterwards. The next time we went to New York, we took the bus.

Party On

While residing in Cinnaminson, my wife was heavily involved with St. Charles Borromeo, the Catholic Church in town. For many years, on New Years' eve, we would attend a party hosted by the Knights of Columbus. It was a great time with many couples from the church attending the affair. They served hot roast beef and pork sandwiches, had a band or a DJ, and served beer and soda.

Every year we had a table with 3-4 couples from the neighborhood. Our table usually included Russ and Carole Waite, who lived next door, Joe and Helen Lehman, from two doors down, the Tedeschi's, Gert and Leo, a retired couple who lived across the street, and the Mondays'.

The New Year's Eve parties were a tradition at St. Charles. It was an event we looked forward to every year. However, due to the excesses demonstrated by some overzealous partygoers and the need for extra insurance the affair was discontinued. For the next two years we went to a friend's house for a small party on New Year's Eve. It just wasn't quite the same.

Then, the following year I saw an advertisement in the local paper for a New Year's Party at the Smithville Inn which was about 50 miles away. There was no cover charge, and you could order anything on the menu. We had always liked our meals at Smithville and thought it would be something different. We talked our neighbor's, the Lehman's, into going with us, not like they were really "party animals."

We got babysitters for the night and headed to Smithville at about 9:00 pm. The drive was just over an hour from Cinnaminson. We always took the backway off the White Horse Pike, through the pine barrens, passed a black Jewish community, the only one I had ever heard of, and an abandoned nike missile battery.

Upon arriving out of the woods, we parked the car and went in. Since we had reservations, we were seated right away. At the table were small hats and noisemakers for each of us. After studying the menu, the polite server took our drink and food orders. Since it had been a workday, we didn't have much to say except small talk about the neighborhood.

It was tough just keeping awake. When our meals arrived, we quickly ate them and listened to the music of a small band playing near us. As the clock slowly moved toward midnight, we decided to call it a night as we had another hour drive to make it home.

As I remember it, the ride felt much longer, like it would never end and Cinnaminson was a thousand miles away. I had to open the driver's side window to keep awake as all the other passengers: my wife, Terry, and Joe and Helen were all fast asleep. Somehow, we made it. After that experience we decided to keep all our New Years' celebrations local unless we could find an autopilot.

Sunday Nights with Mastori's

New Jersey is well-known for its diners. For many years you didn't have to travel far to find a good one. One of our favorite diners was Mastoris' in Bordentown, NJ at the crossroads of Routes 130 and 206. Just outside of Trenton, Mastoris' was the place where many state politicians met and transacted business. Many wedding receptions were held there. It was also a regular stop for many a tourbus. The place even had its own highway entrance on Route 206 South. Jersey politics, I guess.

We used to stop at Mastoris' on Sunday nights after a trip to New Hope or Peddlers Village in Pennsylvania. It was a grand diner. Walking in the front door, you were surrounded by smells and treats from the in-house bakery. There were breads, cookies, cakes, and pies. Almost any flavor you could imagine. The sights and smells were mesmerizing.

If there was a line, you put your name on the "waitlist" as this place was always busy. Once your name was called after registering, you were taken to a booth or table somewhere within the massive facility. We preferred the bar area if there was an open booth. It offered large, comfortable cushioned seats with plenty of room and attentive service. Once seated you were handed a 10-page menu with more than 100 items listed in 8-point type. When the waiter brought you water it was accompanied by a plate of warm cheese and cinnamon breads.

The portions served were typical for a "real" diner, large, hot, and tasty. However, this majestic eatery is now a memory as of 2021. As I understand it, the year before the COVID-19 pandemic, the family sold it to a group of local investors, who primarily looked at profit and loss. The pandemic didn't help the situation. So, on January 1, 2022, Mastori's moved to the status of legend.

The Car Genie from Monday's Corner

Buying a car can be a frustrating experience. You would think it should be a wonderful and joyous occasion, but after you do your homework, shop around, and finally agree on a price you often wonder if you really got a good deal. This is true almost always. I can't imagine buying a car online. You have to see it, sit in it, drive it and "kick the tires."

My wife hates to go car shopping. More often than not the salesman will talk to me rather than her, even though she's buying the vehicle.

Wouldn't it be great if you had a genie like Aladdin's who could grant you the perfect car you wished for without all the hassle, and get you another one when your needs changed? We had such a genie for several years and he granted us more than three wishes.

It all started when I met a neighbor up the street by the name of Bob Monday. He was a great guy. Bob was born in a place called Monday's Corner, near Johnstown, PA. He was very handy and always remodeling his house. When working on a remodel Bob would always write the measurements on his pants so he would have them in front of him. Bob was married to Georgia. We were fast friends for many years. When we went out for dinner, Georgia would always order a child's portion.

The couple often joked about when they had sex. Georgia would say she would be reading the newspaper during the encounter and Bob was supposed to let her know when he was done. From this experience, you could judge that Bob and Georgia's marriage wouldn't last. It wasn't long before they divorced. Bob had two more marriages after that and a child with each before he died at age seventy

As it turned out, Bob was the leasing manager for McGowan Ford, an auto dealership in Ardmore, PA. Bob could get me any car I wanted on a lease deal. He could also get me out of a car if I didn't like it. It was like magic.

For years I leased the cars I wanted or could afford to drive through Bob without any of the hassle. The cars included a top of the line, powder blue Pontiac Bonneville with a moonroof, a sporty, two-door Chevy Monte Carlo, a white Audi, a silver and red Buick Riviera, a red Oldsmobile 88, and a white Acura Legend.

When Bob left the business after his second divorce to pursue his second love, home remodeling, my genie was gone. I was forced to go back to my old ways of going into a dealership and negotiating for the car I wanted to the best of my abilities. To this day I keep searching for that magic bottle on the beach hoping to find another genie.

The Game Plan

Being a life-long Phillies fan, in a constant love-hate relationship with the team, I had an opportunity to purchase season tickets in the late 1970's when the team was in contention for a pennant. I convinced three friends, Larry Brown, Neal Cupersmith, and Nate Rosenblatt, to come in with me on two 16 game plans with four seats per game on the lower level, under cover, at Veteran's stadium along the first-base line. The idea was that each of us would get 8 games during the season with 4 seats per game.

To divide up the tickets evenly and fairly so that everyone could get to see some of the better teams like the Dodgers, St. Louis, and the Giants, the plan was to get together for dinner and pick our games. This way everyone would have an opportunity to pick the games and teams they wanted. For the first two years, when the Phillies were winning, it was great. We even had the opportunity to purchase playoff tickets. However, the seats we were given for those games were in nosebleed heaven at the top of the stadium.

As the Phillies' winning seasons declined, so did the interest in going to the games. The guys didn't want to meet to divide up the tickets. I remember two of them saying, "I can't make it. Just send me my tickets." Human nature being what it is, those of us who met, took the best games and sent the other tickets we didn't want to the non-meeting attendees.

As the team tanked, you couldn't give the tickets away, even for free. It wasn't long before the game plan fell apart, and no one was interested in going. When the time to renew came around the following year, we didn't pick up the option.

Chapter 4: Behind the Camera

I've worked on hundreds of crazy projects during my career as a writer, producer, and photographer. Seldom do things go as planned. Much of what I learned was through trial and error. Hopefully I didn't make the same mistake twice. No matter what happened along the way, I needed to complete the project and make the client happy. My reputation depended upon it. Nobody wanted to hear that you were sorry.

It's often said that you're only as good as your last job. This chapter explores how I got into the audiovisual business, some of my most memorable and challenging projects, and the many different people I worked with along the way.

From Brownies to Nikons and Beyond

It's often been said, "A picture is worth 1000 words." I found that to be true during my career as an audiovisual producer. You just had to be careful what you're shooting. I always had an interest in film and video. I guess that was due to my upbringing from watching TV and going to the movies on Saturday afternoons. As kids we always had those little Brownie cameras around us to take pictures at birthdays and other family events, but I never had a real course in photography. I learned through practice and trial and error. A lot of trial and error.

My first real attempts at photography were in college when taking a master's program in Educational Media. There I learned about composition, film, lighting, and exposure. On our honeymoon in Jamaica, I purchased a Nikon F, my first 35 mm camera. We also bought a Super 8 sound projector, as one of our friends had filmed our wedding in Super 8 that included a soundtrack.

As I began developing articles for different publications like The Philadelphia Inquirer, Design Magazine – a publication for art teachers, and others that required photos, I quickly learned from my mistakes. It led me to building my own copy stand for artwork and purchasing a portable professional lighting kit for on- location photography.

On location, I quickly learned that film was cheap, and that it paid to take multiple shots at different exposures. Capture it on the first trip, not the second. I was well-known at the local photo supply house for purchasing bricks (20 rolls) of 35mm slide film at one time.

I trained myself to carefully look through the viewfinder and become aware of all the surroundings. You only have to see a trash can or candy wrapper once in what would have been a great shot to be alert for distractions in future work. Sometimes I would use a polaroid shot first to check the scene. That was in the days before digital photography.

As my skills and experience improved, I was able to promote myself as an industrial photographer and handled a wide range of on-location assignments in business and education for my own projects as well as other clients including Atlantic Electric Company, Charming Shoppes, Mannington Mills, The National Maritime Safety Association, and Philadelphia International Airport. Many of my slides became part of the AECT stock photo collection for educational use.

In addition to 35mm photography, I experimented with Super 8 film. My first motion picture camera was a Bolex 155 Macrozoom. It was an amazing tool that allowed you to focus as close as one inch. In fact, I still have it. It probably belongs in a museum. I made numerous short films using it and built articles around my work which appeared in *The*

Bolex Reporter and several Super 8 magazines published at that time.

As the media changed, so did I. I went from writing and shooting to more directing and instructional design. I preferred film to digital photography. I know digital is the rage, but I had more fun with film.

Where My Ideas Come From

Ideas come easy for me. Some are great, others not so much. In college, over 60 years ago, we had an assignment to create a product and build an advertising campaign around it. The product I envisioned at the time was "Dissolvo," biodegradable bottles and containers that would quickly and easily dissolve in water. They were ecologically sound. No need to collect or dump them in landfills. Today there are similar products coming to market.

Here's another one. The "Barbie Doll." No, I don't claim I invented it, but I did have an idea for a version of a "Barbie." I called it "Uh, Oh Barbie." It was a pregnant doll with a baby included. I jokingly talked about it on the beach one year. Someone must have overheard my discussion, because before long there was one on the market.

Throughout my career, clients hired me for my creative ideas and approaches. I've often been asked where my creative ideas came from. Someone once told me that creativity is looking at the same thing others look at but seeing something different. That was often the case with me. I also adapted themes or concepts from something I had heard or watched. Quite often, if someone described a project to me, I could quickly come up with a creative way to effectively carry it through to an audience. I accomplished that successfully many times. And I must admit that I reused the same theme or idea with different audiences and industries.

Here are a few examples. In the late 1960's there was an academy award winning short film called "Why Man Creates" produced by Saul Bass Productions. It contained a series of vignettes focused on creative ideas. The opening segment was called, "The Edifice." Using animation, it visually described the evolution of man and civilization from the earliest days through modern life, in about two minutes. The beginning piece showing cavemen working together to trap a mammoth stuck in my mind. A few years later, when tasked with developing a program on "Union Organizing", that opening sequence seemed to fit. It worked and I reused it successfully several times after that for other clients. Sometimes you don't have to reinvent the wheel, just change the vehicle you're driving. I'm not the only one to modify or tweak ideas. Hollywood does it all the time. If you've ever watched the introduction to "The Big Bang Theory," they use an adaptation of "The Edifice."

Several years ago, I was doing a pharmaceutical training program on a vaginal product designed to help bring on delivery by pregnant women in the hospital. What popped into my mind was a scene from the movie "Patch Adams" with Robin Williams where he was charged with welcoming a group of gynecologists to the medical school. He covered the doorway to the building with a replica of a giant vagina.

The doctors had to walk through it to enter the building. When the team leader asked why I was smiling, I told the group. A wasted idea.

Over the years I've used a wide range of themes and concepts depending upon the project. Some include: "Mission Impossible," "The Amazing Race," treasure hunts, the Olympics, famous characters throughout history, like George Washington, Ben Franklin, General George Patton and Indiana Jones, or variations of them. One theme that almost all companies love is, "The Secret to Our Success."

When I was approached to do a program on accounting, which can be dull, I created a cartoon character, Numbers O'Toole, to make the program more interesting to the audience. He not only imparted knowledge and wisdom, but a little humor along the way. The organization used this character for more than 20 years. For another program on a similar subject, I used George Washington. He came to life out of a dollar bill to present the topic.

For an audio cassette company, I created a sales presentation with the announcer inside the sampler. He briefly described the various uses of cassettes for sales and training, and the quality of this one.

When I created a program on Parliamentary Procedures for one organization, with a few changes, I was able to sell it to several others.

When working with nonprofits, like charities, which almost always had low-budgets, I developed a template I could use over and over again for yearly tributes and fundraising purposes. It provided work and also allowed me to quickly produce a professional product. The same was true for a host of educational programs I created for federally validated innovative programs in New Jersey. The templates and the formula I created were the secret to my success.

Don't Mess with the Marines

For several months in 1970, I worked for the Boeing Company's Vertol Division developing helicopter audiovisual maintenance training programs for the US Navy's Sea Knight helicopters, used by the Marine Corps. What I found interesting was that the maintenance instructions for the helicopters were designed by aeronautical engineers. Tech reps taught the Marine mechanics how to perform them. However, the Marines had their own way of doing things. And our scripts followed the Marines' approach. Once the scripts were approved, we would go on site to Quantico, Virginia to shoot visuals for the programs.

At the time, my family had a Ford Fairlane 500, which I drove to Quantico. The company paid 9 cents a mile for travel, plus an additional 1 cent per mile, for each passenger you took along. On one particular trip I went on location with another writer/producer in the training group, Fred Reed. Fred was a big man, about 6 foot four and he weighed about 250 pounds. I always thought I should have gotten at least 2 cents a mile for taking him with me, but rules were rules.

Where we shot our stills was near the hangars where the presidential helicopter fleet, Marine Corp. Helicopter Squadron 1 is stationed. You weren't allowed to point your cameras in that direction, or a military policeman (MP) would come over and take the film out of your camera or worse.

When we were on assignment, it was required to check in with the plant once a day to give them a status report. On that trip, I couldn't help myself. When I reported in, I told them that Fred had been photographing Marine Squadron 1 and been caught by an MP. Not wanting the MP to confiscate his film, Fred decked the guard and was in the brig as a result. I really had them going. Then I told them the truth.

Mission Impossible

One of the first freelance assignments I took after being laid off from the Boeing Company in 1970, was developing a slide/sound presentation for the New Jersey Council for Environmental Education. I received the lead about the project from my friend Dan DeSantis, a media specialist at the South Jersey Educational Improvement Center (EIC).

The Council was based at Montclair State University, more than 100 miles from my home in Cinnaminson, but I had nothing to lose, except some gas and my time. So, I made an appointment with the director of the project and drove up to Montclair for a morning meeting. It was a good, long ride north, up the New Jersey Turnpike, then out the Garden State Parkway to an exit in the 160's. The trip took about two hours.

Upon arriving at the school, I met with the director, Dr. Edward Ambry, and his team. The organization wanted to develop an awareness presentation they could show to different audiences about the goals of the Council and the services they offered to school districts and civic organizations around the state. They had a limited budget, as most state-related organizations do, and needed it completed in about six weeks. Having a lot of time on my hands, I agreed to do the job.

Following my normal development process, I asked for all the print and visual materials they had describing their vision, services, plans and contact information. They supplied me with some brochures and slides, and I went to work developing a concept and a script. Thinking about what TV programs were popular at the time, and what might be a great attention getter for opening the presentation, I settled on "Mission Impossible."

I built the opening around a scene on the Garden State Parkway, where an "agent" pulls off the road, goes to a phone booth, picks up the phone and hears that well-known message, "Your mission is to... If you choose to accept it...This message will self-destruct in ten seconds." The client loved it.

Any artwork needed for the program, I drew myself. Knowing a professional narration would help carry the script, I contacted another friend, Bob Donze, who was still at Boeing, to record the narration. Bob had a good voice and had been an announcer on the Temple University radio station.

Once the script was approved, I went around the state taking slides to match. I also took shots for the program opening in a phone booth off the parkway. The end result was a 10-minute program the Council was happy with. They got their monies' worth. I was even offered a position with the group, but to travel that distance every day was too much, a real mission impossible.

The Commerce Business Daily

Throughout my 50-plus years in the field of communications I've played many roles. I've been a writer, director, photographer, producer, instructional designer, salesman, and even an artist from time to time. What was interesting to learn along the way was that many of the production companies I worked with, even large ones, didn't have writers on staff. They had salesmen, editors, photographers, and assistants, but few if any writers.

This was a real learning experience and one that helped me to survive in the ever-changing world of media. When I started my own company, ZM Squared, in 1970, I looked in all directions for possible work. One search, using the old-fashioned Philadelphia yellow pages, led me to a company called Animation Arts, a film and animation production house located in the city. Through constant monthly calls, I hooked up with Animation Arts to write the first promotional audiovisual presentation for the Express Mail program, and that service offered by the U.S. Postal Service is still around today.

During my work on the script, the company's owner, Harry Ziegler, told me how he found out about the project. He subscribed to a weekly publication called The Commerce Business Daily (CBD). It listed all types of projects coming up for bid as well as government auctions. It wasn't long before I too was subscribing to the publication.

Within a couple of weeks of receiving The Daily, I saw a bid listing for a production project being offered for bid by The Philadelphia School District, where I received my basic education. The project was for developing a series of career awareness programs for the district's Clerical Skills Laboratory.

I figured my costs for the project, submitted a bid, and won part of the contract. My portion of the job would be developing three filmstrips focused on clerical occupations: Typist, Office Machine Operator, and Office Worker. The other part of the contract was won by H.G. Peters, a well-known film production company located in Primos, Delaware County. They were awarded a contract to produce 2 motion pictures: Pocketbook Percentages and Office Workflow.

As I began work on my programs, H.G. Peters reached out to me. They wanted to know if I was interested in writing the scripts for their two films. I thought it was odd at the time. I had chased this company early in my career for work with no success. They didn't need me before, but now they did. Since I was creating scripts on closely related topics, I accepted the assignment and wrote the scripts.

I never did win another project from those listed in the CBD, nor did I work for H.G. Peters again. However, I continued my subscription for many years. It proved to me that you never know where jobs can come from.

Perceived Necessity

It is often said, "Necessity is the mother of invention." You can see attempts at that on shows like "Shark Tank," where folks think they have invented "a better mousetrap." In the late 1970's, before the era of video, I thought I had an idea for a "better trap."

At the time, Encyclopedia Britannica Corporation offered a series of short, 8mm single-concept films on different careers to schools across the country. These were 3–5-minute films with no sound. After watching several, I came up with an idea to improve them by adding a soundtrack to each, explaining what the viewer was seeing. I thought adding a voiceover narration would add value and interest to each presentation.

Not seeing any downside to the idea. I researched the company's departments and wrote to the person in charge of new educational products and explained my approach. To my surprise, Encyclopedia Britannica was willing to do a test and pay for it. Based on our discussions, I selected 4 career films from their catalogue. These were Bricklayers, Carpenters, Electricians, and Plumbers and Pipefitters.

With the company's approval I studied each career based on the film content and wrote a script to match the action of each. Then I produced the soundtracks using a professional narrator and included appropriate background music. Each track explained what the viewer was seeing and described the career.

The company was happy with the test. However, it was just at the time when mediums and technologies were changing and moving towards video tape, so we never got beyond the test stage. But I can honestly say I had done work for Encyclopedia Britannica Corporation.

Ted Knight is at the Front Door

Early on, when I started my production company, I narrated my own programs. However, I knew if I was going to succeed in this business my final products were going to require a professional narration. A professional voice and background music can often hide or overcome any number of problems.

As the name of my company and its services spread throughout the area, I received a call from a narrator named Larry Brown. Larry had been a radio DJ for many years. He also did voiceover work on one of the local TV channels, was the voice for a local car dealership, as well as for a national weight-loss company. In fact, one of his on-camera commercials regularly appeared in Dick Clark's commercial blooper specials.

Larry volunteered to come to my home office in Cinnaminson, NJ for an interview and audition. I agreed. When he arrived, he was wearing a sports jacket and tie, and carrying an umbrella. As he entered the house, my wife, Terry, was coming down the stairs. Looking at Larry, she thought Ted Knight from the Mary Tyler Moore Show was in the house. He was like Ted's double: the hair, the jacket, the tie, the umbrella, and the voice. The hair I later learned was a series of different length toupees which he would change weekly.

Larry and I chatted for a while. Then I gave him the draft scripts of several programs I was working on to look over and read. He had a great voice, one that could help to capture an audience's attention. He could sound knowledgeable, caring, or sympathetic, depending upon the mood of the script.

Larry and I formed a friendship that lasted many years. I would go to his home studio in Cheltenham, PA and direct his narrations as he recorded them. Larry also edited the audio and was able to add background music if needed. He introduced me to a number of retail and nonprofit clients he knew. I, on the other hand, brought numerous education projects to the table. We developed a fine-tuned process. I would write the scripts and photograph them. Larry would do the narration and music. Experience with these different types of clients enabled me to grow and expand my base and provided Larry with on-going voiceover work.

However, one problem arose that almost destroyed the relationship. One of my clients was a labor union based in Washington, DC. I was doing a series of officer training programs. For some reason, Larry was unable to say the word "officer." It came out as "ossifer." And the client picked that up immediately. As much as he tried, Larry just couldn't say "officer." As a result, I couldn't use him on any of those programs. Luckily, there were other clients and voiceover projects to be had.

Larry and I remained friends above it all for many years, even after I left the production end of the business.

The Swashbuckling Photographer

As a young boy, I was fascinated by sailing ships. I loved watching seafaring movies like Captain Blood with Errol Flynn and Captain Horatio Hornblower with Gregory Peck. In weekend art classes I drew many a sailing ship and imagined what life was like years ago on the high seas. However, when I did venture out on the ocean, I got seasick. In fact, on family fishing trips, they brought me along to chum.

Now, during my career as a writer/producer one of the most interesting and challenging assignments I had was developing a series of audiovisual training programs on the International Rules of the Road for the International Organization of Masters, Mates and Pilots (IOMMP) based in Linthicum Heights, Maryland. These are the highly trained folks that safely pilot the big ships, like tankers and freighters, into harbors around the country. To gain some nautical experience, it was suggested I go onboard a ship for several days. In spite of my fear of seasickness I went with a large bottle of Dramamine.

The adventure began early on a Monday morning. My father, Louie, picked me up at my home in Cinnaminson, NJ and drove me down to Bridgeport, NJ to catch a ride on a 660-foot chemical tanker named the Edgar M. Queeny. I had always thought ships were named after women: boy was I wrong.

As mentioned in earlier stories, I really didn't like riding with my father, but our sons were very young at the time and my wife couldn't leave them that early in the morning. Luckily the ride to Bridgeport was uneventful and I thanked my father for the transportation.

Upon boarding the ship, I met the captain, William Roberts, a man in his early 50's who didn't look anything like Errol Flynn. I also met several members of the crew. They were friendly and I explained why I was there. I also promised to stay out of the way. What I quickly learned about this ship was that it was completely made of metal and extremely noisy all day and all night long. Between the engines and the vibrations there was no peace and quiet. Being a light sleeper didn't help the situation.

The first night out we traveled down the Chesapeake and ran into a major storm. The metal tanker bounced and rolled all that night, and so did I. It brought to mind the song by folk singer Gordon Lightfoot about the Edmund Fitzgerald that sank on Lake Superior. Luckily, by morning the storm had passed and the ship and I were still afloat. For the next few days, I stayed on deck most of the time photographing passing ships displaying different signal flags and markings.

At mealtime, I ate in the galley with the crew. The food wasn't bad, and I learned to eat things I wasn't accustomed to. You eat what they give you and don't complain. During the nights onboard I tried to shut out the noise and vibrations but wasn't very successful. Thank heaven it was only a three-day trip. On the third day we docked at Bridgeport, CT. Once leaving the ship and kissing the ground, I caught a cab to the Bridgeport train station, caught a southbound Amtrak and traveled back to Philly and then home. Mission accomplished.

Based on my visuals and some additional artwork, I assembled a sample slide presentation for the IOMMP to demonstrate what a training program on The Rules would look like. The company I was producing this for ended up with the project and seven programs.

About a year later, in January of 1975, I saw on the news that the Edgar M. Queeny, loaded with petroleum products and chemicals had collided with another ship, the Corinthos, on the Delaware River below Chester, PA. The Queeny suffered only minor damage, but the Corinthos was destroyed. I'm glad I wasn't aboard for that experience.

Ready When You Are C.B.

In the early 1980's I was hired to develop a series of slide/sound programs for the International Masonry Institute (IMI), a training branch for the Bricklayers and Allied Craftsmen Union, based at the time in Washington, D.C. The director of the organization, Bruce V, wanted to produce programs on basic bricklaying techniques and he wanted to shoot them in Utah, where he was from. I had no problem with that since the client was paying for the travel. Bruce told me he would meet my team on site in Utah on an agreed-upon date right after President's weekend. I told Bruce that if there were any problems to call me before we left for Utah. That was a long way to go and there were costs involved.

Planning for the trip was important. I had written scripts for each program and Bruce had approved them prior to the shoot. I learned early in the production business that it always pays to have a backup photographer with you on a major shoot out of town just in case there was something wrong with one of the cameras or the film. The chance that both cameras would fail was very small. However, it didn't pay to take chances. Nobody wants to hear that you're sorry if something goes wrong. Plus, it was a long way to go for a "do over."

My approach to the situation was based on a story I once heard about Cecil B. DeMille, a famous director of epic films like "The Ten Commandments," "The Buccaneer," and "The Greatest Show on Earth." It seems DeMille was filming a major chariot battle scene and had cameras set up in several different locations. After the action had taken place, DeMille went around to the different camera positions and asked what they were able to film. When he went to the first station, the camera operator explained that his camera had broken down just as the battle started. Undeterred, DeMille went to the next position. Here, the cameraman said all he got was dust because of the way the wind was blowing. When DeMille got to the third location, the camera operator said, "Ready when you are C.B." So, to avoid a similar situation I hired a good friend and experienced photographer, Dan DeSantis, to go along with me. Dan and I had worked on numerous projects together. I trusted him, his camera, and his judgment.

With our cameras, plenty of film, and approved scripts in hand, my team headed out on President's weekend for our 5-day shoot in Utah. We flew from Philadelphia to Dallas/Fort Worth and then changed planes for a flight to Salt Lake City. When we landed in Salt Lake, we rented a car and drove three hours to the IMAT training center in a place called Weber Canyon. There we were greeted by the training director, Bill Walters, a grizzled veteran of bricklaying, who upon our arrival told us Bruce wasn't coming after all and the shoot was off. It was a case of I was ready, and Bruce wasn't. He wasn't even there.

Dan and I looked at each other in amazement. We couldn't believe it. I then turned to Mr. Walters and said, "Look, we're here for five days and we're going to shoot the program with or without Bruce." And that's what we did. Bill contacted another IMI employee from the center, Jim Thomas, who acted as our model demonstrating the correct way to lay brick and block and build corners. Important skills for professional bricklayers. We shot each program, step-by-step, according to the script.

After several days, we completed the onsite work and returned to Jersey. We had the film processed and I assembled the programs in slide trays according to the scripts. I then made an appointment with Bruce in D.C. to show him the results of our efforts. I also charged him $600.00 for coming to D.C. and continued to do that on every trip to the organization's offices. I felt my time was worth it.

I completed several other projects for IMI after that, including teaching IMI instructors how to create their own training videos. Eventually the IMI established a national training center in Bowie, Maryland and completed similar projects inhouse.

History is Rewritten by the Winners

Ben Franklin once commented that history is written by the winners. I saw that firsthand while writing an orientation program for a large chain of women's clothing stores based in the Philadelphia area.

Several times a year, during the late 1980's and early 1990's, I would write and produce 16mm sound filmstrip programs to introduce the latest fashions to the store associates around the country. These were 12 to 15-minute shows utilizing the delivery medium of the day, LaBelle projectors.

To make the presentations more exciting and capture the audience I would use a current topic or character in the show. Sometimes it was the Olympics; if it was the right year, Christmas, or a popular conceit like Max Headroom, a TV character of bygone times. I was also tasked with developing recruiting programs and a history of the company.

This chain, originally called Charming Shoppes, was founded by two sets of brothers in Norristown PA around the late 1940's. As the company grew the name of the stores were changed to Fashion Bug, a more exciting and popular moniker.

When I wrote the first orientation program for the company, I was told about the history and families running the company by the then president. When he and his brother retired, I was asked to revise the program based on the historical view of the other set of brothers still involved in the management of the organization. It reminded me of when I did a program on how cable TV operates and interviewed two different engineers of a well-known cable company. Each gave me their understanding of how cable works. They were totally different.

Scratch My Back

You never know where business will come from. I received a call one day in the early 1990's from one of the owners of the Viking Yacht company, Bob Healey. Viking, based in New

Gretna, New Jersey, produces some of the finest and most expensive custom boats in the world.

Mr. Healey told me he had a charity he was working with in South America called Living Bridges and needed a 35 mm sound/slide presentation for fundraising purposes. He added that if it proved successful, he would hire me to produce several sales videos for the yacht company. That was extra motivation on my end.

I met with Bob at his home in Lumberton, NJ and discussed the project. I also asked to review what materials he had that we could use in the presentation like slides and brochures. That would affect the price for the program. I also explained the process I used to create such a presentation. Based on our meeting, I wrote a sales proposal including the estimated price for the project.

Mr. Healey accepted my proposal, and I went to work creating the fundraising program based on his needs and using the available materials. Based on my previous experiences developing programs of this nature, I knew that having an experienced professional narrator, who could deliver an empathetic reading of the script would greatly help to sell the need for funds, and I had just the pro – Larry Brown. Larry had involved me in the production of numerous non-profit presentations, and I knew he could deliver the care and loving feeling needed in this one.

Using the visuals supplied by Bob Healey, along with several computer-generated graphic slides, music from my stock library, and Larry's voiceover, I was able to create an effective, tear-jerking presentation that helped to raise needed funds for the charity. As a result, I was hired to produce several presentations for Viking during the 1990's, but that's another whale of a tale.

The Rare Book You Can't Buy a Copy Of

No, I'm not talking about a first edition of the Gutenberg Bible or "A Tale of Two Cities. However, if you go online and look up my name, one of the books listed on Amazon.com is "Powerful Presentations" by Peter Zakroff. But you can't get a copy of it, as there's only one and I have it. No, it wasn't banned by a school district, a nasty librarian who didn't like the content, or even a dissatisfied client.

Here's the story. Early in 1991 my writing and production business was very slow. It was like a mini- depression around Philadelphia and I was searching for additional sources of revenue. My friend, Nate Rosenblatt, worked with a company named Round Lake Publishing developing a series of books containing samples of stock business letters and legal documents. Having written a wealth of stock scripts for AV productions on almost every topic you could imagine, like company orientations, new product introductions, and nonprofits, I approached the publisher with an idea for creating a book of sample scripts, with suggested narrations and visuals that people in business, industry, and education could use as models for writing and producing their own programs on these topics. I went up to Connecticut where Round Lake was based and presented my approach to the publisher. He agreed to pay me $4000 plus a royalty for each book sold.

Having a contract in hand, I went to work revising scripts I had written on the most requested topics. These included awareness, basic retail selling skills, new hire orientations, sales presentations, fund raising, tributes, and more.

I opened the book with instructions for proposing a presentation to a client including the goals and objectives of the project, features, and benefits, as well as an outline of the content, which I called "Defining the Subject." This was followed by a chapter on scriptwriting basics. Next, I provided different examples of successful approaches I had used for starting presentations. These included using cartoon characters, the documentary approach, historical openings and famous persons, as well as "take-offs" or conceits of well-known movies like "Indiana Jones" or events such as the Olympics.

Then I offered chapters covering company stories or corporate image presentations that could be adapted to any size organization, non-profit scripts for charities and tributes to donors, recruiting programs, orientation and training models, educational awareness models, as well as different types of sales presentations covering new product introductions, real estate, and insurance. The final chapter of the book showed the reader how to put it all together. It covered topics like artwork, talent acquisition, equipment, and music.

In its entirety, the book was some 500 pages in length and included more than 35 complete scripts with draft narrations and suggested visuals for each. It went through five drafts performed by my mentor, Val Udell.

When the final draft was completed more than a year later, I was met with disappointment. Though I was paid for writing the book, Round Lake decided not to publish it and I was given the rights to publish it myself. They just were not sure where to sell it. Over the years I've explored different ideas for getting the book published in some shape or form. This included putting it on compact disc, breaking the book into three separate texts, and making the scripts available on a website. However, at the present time, the only complete copy sits on my bookshelf waiting to be reinvented.

Let's Kill All the Lawyers

Early in 1992, lawyer jokes were all the rage. Everyday there was at least one new joke or cartoon in the newspaper or being repeated by friends or acquaintances. Books full of lawyer jokes were popping up all over.

Seizing upon the craze, I decided to try something a little different, a calendar for 1993. My idea was to produce a 12-month, 11 x 17 two-color, desk or wall calendar. Each month would have an illustration of the punchline to a well-known lawyer joke, such as "Lawyers are the easiest people to operate on. No heart, no guts and the mouth and the butt are interchangeable," or "Question: How can you tell the difference between a dead skunk and a lawyer in the road?

Answer: There are skid marks in front of the skunk." In addition, for each month there would be different assignments, like "go to ethics class," "ethics class canceled," "hang out at a busy intersection," or "practice talking out of both sides of your mouth."

To create the artwork for each month and construct the calendar I tapped my artist friend, Dick Louderback. Dick was great at drawing cartoons, and I had worked with him for many years. He always had dreams of publishing his own cartoon strip in a newspaper, but that never materialized.

To attract customer attention in stores the front cover introduced the product with the title, The 1993 Legal Calendar and had a tagline, "12 months of laughs at attorneys, barristers, counselors, lawyers, mouthpieces or whatever you choose to call them." To visually enhance the cover we added an illustration of William Shakespeare and his famous line from King Henry VI, Part II, "The first thing we do, let's kill all the lawyers."

Once Dick had completed the drawings I worked with a local printer, Norm Wahner, of South Jersey Printing, to run several hundred copies of the calendar and shrink-wrap them. I promoted the calendar through a wire service and press releases. I also contacted area stores and chains that carried calendars. I was able to place a large number of calendars in several Border's bookstores. I also had a great news article in a local business paper and did a radio interview on a local radio station.

It was a fun project, and I garnered some good publicity, learned a great deal about promotion, but in the end the monetary return wasn't enough to do it again. It was one and done.

Everybody Wants to be a Star

One thing I've learned over the years is to never deal with the friends of relatives when it comes to the production business. This is all based on a personal and aggravating experience. It's a little different than having a friend or relative in the retail business who can get you a deal on an appliance, what I call "The theory of relativity."

This disaster started at a family affair. It was the wedding for Christine, the daughter of one of my wife's uncles. We called him Cheyenne. He was a big, strong, handsome guy in the construction business and reminded you of Clint Walker, who played Cheyenne on the television show by the same name. Cheyenne knew I produced industrial videos and cornered me at the affair. It seems he had a friend, Anthony, who wanted to produce a twelve-to-fifteen-minute video on repairing small boats. It was supposed to be like Bill Villa's "This Old House," but for boats. Wanting to remain on his good side, I told Cheyenne to have his friend contact me.

I received a call from Anthony a few days later and agreed to meet with him one morning at a small boat yard on the Delaware River just off Route 95 below the Philadelphia Airport. Anthony described what he wanted to accomplish, and I explained the production process. After the meeting I wrote up a proposal for the project, complete with the timing and price for producing his project. Anthony explained what funds he had available to make the video. This was not going to be an extravaganza. In my proposal I spelled out the steps involved which included writing a script, having him review and approve it. Then we would start filming. After the filming we would edit the footage and create a final product. Anthony signed the proposal and sent me a deposit for one-half of the project cost as agreed.

After receiving the signed proposal and the deposit, I drafted a rough script based on his input and reviewed it with him. Then we set up a date and decided on the location to do the shooting. It was the same site where we originally met along the Delaware. I also explained to Anthony what to wear to make the best impression on screen. I also recruited a videographer from Aldon Productions in Berlin, NJ to film while I directed the production. I had worked with Aldon before on several projects and they were nice to work with and reasonable, especially since this was a low budget project.

On the morning of the shoot, Anthony met us at the boatyard with the craft he wanted to use in the program. Using the draft script, we worked for several hours filming the project. Anthony was not exactly dressed as a presenter. In fact, we had to lend him a belt for his pants. All day long Anthony wanted to do things his way, while I tried to explain to him that we needed to repeat certain steps to get different angles.

After the shoot, the team at Aldon edited the video based on the script and prepared a final product for Anthony to view.

The second payment was due on completion of the filming so I could pay Aldon for their work. Anthony kept delaying the payment and giving different excuses. In addition, he wanted the master tapes. After much back and forth, Anthony said he would drop off a final check at Aldon if he could pick up the masters there. I agreed but told Aldon to only accept a certified check from Anthony as I didn't trust him.

Long story short, Aldon gave the masters to Anthony. He gave Aldon a personal check made out to my business, and it bounced higher than a rubber ball. It was the only time in my more than fifty years of being in business that someone did that to me. I vowed to never let it happen again.

The Credits

I always get a kick watching the credits at the end of a motion picture or television show, seeing how many different people were used to complete the project. Besides the cast, and the four or five production companies that may have been involved in the project, they list the director, assistant director, producer, executive producer, another executive producer, casting director, key grip, second key grip, electrician, sound editor, first unit on-location director, second unit on-location director, food service, makeup, transportation coordinator, key actors' secretaries, and so on, right down to who supplied the portable potties.

I spent most of my life writing and producing industrials and educational programs. For many of those projects I did almost everything, kind of a one-man band or production company. I guess I should have listed my name for each of the above-mentioned tasks, but it would have been a little redundant. In most cases I was just happy to get paid.

Chapter 5: Southern Exposure

Horace Greeley, a newspaper editor from the nineteenth century was famous for the saying, "Go west young man." Some 150 years later, in the late summer of 1993, I decided to go south. I accepted a position with NCR Corporation, in Columbia, South Carolina. Prior to relocating there, I had not experienced southern life, except for reading a few magazine articles and a three-hour house tour during my initial job interview. Having grown up in Philadelphia and spending 20 plus years in South Jersey, moving south, let alone to South Carolina, was a completely new and "eye opening" experience.

A Damn Yankee in South Carolina

In the early 1990's the business climate around Philadelphia, PA was depressing. Clients were no longer interested in relationships. It was more about how cheaply they could get a production.

One Sunday morning in the spring of 1993, I saw an advertisement in the *Philadelphia Inquirer* for a multimedia consultant with NCR Corporation in Columbia, South Carolina. Seeking a new challenge, I replied via snail mail and within a week received a call from Pam Jenkins in NCR's Human Resources Department in Columbia. I chatted with Pam about the position. By the end of the call I was asked to come down to their facility in Columbia for face-to-face interviews.

A few days later, I flew into Columbia. At that time there were direct flights between Philly and Columbia. My flight out of Philly International was delayed for an hour by a thunderstorm. By the time I arrived in Columbia it was almost midnight. I rented a car, and after several wrong turns in a place I was totally unfamiliar with, I eventually found my way to the Marriott Courtyard hotel where there was a room waiting for me.

The next morning, I drove to NCR and interviewed with several people, including Liz Pearson, the head of the sales training department, who explained what the company was looking for. I brought along a portfolio to show her samples of work I had done. After that session, I met with Pam, the HR person I had spoken with on the phone. While there, I was also given a drug test. The only drug I had taken was Dramamine, as I was not an experienced flier and wanted to calm my nerves.

Following the interviews, I was taken to lunch at a local Chili's to get acquainted with several current members of the training group. After lunch, a local realtor, Tom Roberts, took me on a house tour of areas surrounding Columbia. Not having been on a job interview in years, this was an interesting experience.

A few weeks later, I was offered a job at the facility in Columbia. Having worked on my own and from a home office for many years, this was going to be life-changing.

My introduction to southern living began with the purchase of a home. In early June NCR gave us a 3-day house hunting tour. My wife and I flew to Columbia, SC. The company put us up in a Hilton Hotel during our stay. Our realtor/guide, Joan Reedy, a sister of the founder of the Vera Bradley company, well-known for attractive bags and travel luggage, showed us tons of houses. Some houses we didn't like from the outside. After a while it almost became a blur. We couldn't remember what we liked and disliked. Eventually we found a beautiful three-year-old brick home just off Lake Murray in Lexington County. We placed a bid on the property and after some haggling back and forth it was ours. A similar house in Jersey would have cost almost twice as much.

I agreed to start work the first week in August of 1993. On a Saturday morning, while my wife and daughter were at the shore, I packed my car and prepared to head to South Carolina for a Monday morning start. I stopped at the local coffee shop on Route 130 in Cinnaminson for a cup of java and a donut and headed south. My plan was to make the trip in 2 days, stopping overnight in Virginia where I had a reservation at a motel just off of Interstate 95. I could then arrive in the Columbia area midday Sunday, where there was temporary housing arranged by NCR at an apartment complex.

About halfway there, I began wondering if I had made the right decision. I told myself I had made a commitment and would do whatever it took to make it work. It was too late to change my mind.

Nine to Five

On that Monday morning in August of 1993 I reported to work at NCR. I first met with Pam Jenkins in Human Resources, and then my boss-to-be, Liz Pearson, the Training Director. What followed was a bunch of new hire protocols, including having my picture taken, and signing on.

I was assigned a cubicle, which for a guy who freelanced from home was very confining. Nearby were several other team members including Freddie Layberger, a computer geek who was always trying to push the technology beyond its capabilities, Carol, a graphic artist, Betsy, a technical writer, and Evelyn, a diehard southerner who did not like change. A few days later, we were joined by another newcomer, Eli Cassorla, from New York, a former IBM employee who had a son working for NCR. Eli was a Jew of Spanish heritage and had that typical New York demeanor, which you either loved or hated.

Before coming to Columbia, I had worked primarily with Apple computers. In my cubicle were two CRT screens attached to the NCR network which was never secured and often went down for hours at a time. One computer I had never seen before and wasn't even sure how it worked. The other was a rudimentary personal computer.

Getting familiar with the people and the equipment was a real learning experience. I again questioned why I had made the move but carried on as I had made a commitment to my family. Every day I would get to work early and stop in the cafeteria for a cup of coffee and a donut. Then, I would go to my cave to see what the tasks were for the day and what I could accomplish.

At lunchtime, I would grab a bite to eat in the cafeteria, and weather permitting, take a walk around the facility's grounds for exercise.

I quickly learned that I was pretty far down on the business chain to make a difference in promoting their products and was not really a highly technical person. I also learned that it was never the Civil War in South Carolina. It was referred to as "The late war of northern aggression." And some folks were still engaged in it.

To keep my spirits up, I joined the company volleyball team which played other organizations in Columbia. I also participated in intramural volleyball which was played after work on the company grounds. The first time I played was just after I arrived at NCR I didn't have any sneakers. Being a dumb Yankee I played in my bare feet and was rudely introduced to fire ants.

Going to work at the same place five days a week was an experience I had not endured for almost 25 years. I was assigned to attend sessions on computer development in this one conference room. It was a long, thin room with gray walls and boring discussions. I couldn't stay there for more than 45 minutes, as it gave me a headache.

The Visual Police

Having been in the communication business most of my life, I'm amazed that some college professors and high-level corporate officers know or care very little about what their audience sees. I saw that firsthand in several instances while working and taking graduate classes in South Carolina. To try and remedy the situations when they arose, I became a member of The Visual Police. Now, we couldn't arrest anyone, as much as we would have liked to, for the crimes of boring people or ruining their eyes. However, we could make suggestions to improve their presentations. Whether they took them or not is another story.

Here's how this visual enforcement team came into existence. While at NCR, I considered going for my doctorate in either Education or Communications since my employer offered tuition reimbursement. With that goal in mind, I enrolled in The University of South Carolina. My first class was a graduate level communications course. It was being taught by Dr. Fried. My class was "live" at the university, but a number of students were taking the course remotely at different locations around the state.

At my first class, I noticed problems with the color backgrounds of the slides and the size of the type being broadcast to the satellite centers. The backgrounds had little contrast with the text, and the type size was too small to be viewed clearly on the television screens being used at the time. Having been involved in developing training and promotional programs for over 20 years, and employed as a multimedia designer at NCR, I didn't think I could sit through a course presented in this manner.

After class, I offered Dr. Fried some suggestions for improving his visuals, which he took. It also turned out that the class materials he was using were inconsistent with my experiences developing effective training. There were different assignments we had to complete during the course. The examples he used did not have a flow from one assignment to another. By the time I completed the course, the instructor's visuals were much more readable on the screen, and he was using my work as the examples for flow from one assignment to another in his future classes.

Not everyone takes helpful advice. In another situation, one of the corporate officers at NCR was preparing a major policy presentation to the plant workforce. He was going to deliver his entire talk using a single PowerPoint slide covered with text of all different sizes. It was horrible as well as unreadable. I suggested he break up his presentation into several slides in order for his audience to be able to clearly see his key points. His quick response to me was, "No! I'll just make the screen bigger."

The Emerald Dragon

When we moved to South Carolina, our second car was a Pontiac Station Wagon. The wagon was on its last wheels and needed replacement. My wife was interested in a Ford

Explorer. After work one evening we traveled to a nearby Ford dealership in Columbia to look at what they had in stock. A model that caught Terry's attention was an emerald green Explorer sitting out front on the dealer's lot. After a short test drive to ensure that was what she wanted, we settled into a price negotiation for the vehicle.

Apparently, the salesman wasn't accustomed to dealing with Yankees. We went round and round on the value of the Pontiac as a trade-in. They kept upping the value of the wagon in order to make a deal. We kept trying to get them to lower the price of the Explorer. The discussion seemed to go on for hours. In fact, they closed the dealership for the night with us still in negotiations with the salesman and his manager. Near exhaustion, we finally made a deal that made both sides happy.

A Southern Style Thanksgiving

Living in Columbia, we realized it was too much to drive back to New Jersey for Thanksgiving. With a 16-hour drive each way, we felt we would be on the road more than off and completely worn out by the end of the return trip.

We decided on a different plan of action. Why not go further south to Hilton Head Island? It was only a few hours' drive from Columbia. We could rent a condominium and spend the weekend there from Wednesday afternoon to Sunday. After reviewing several travel brochures, we called The Sea Pines Plantation in Hilton Head, which was located near the ocean and rented a two-bedroom condo for four nights. Since it was the off-season, the price was very reasonable.

On that Wednesday afternoon, I left work a little early, and after our daughter, Laura, got out of school, we loaded up the car and drove to Sea Pines. Upon our arrival, just after dark, we checked in at the rental office and received a key to a nearby condominium where we hoped to spend the next few days relaxing and enjoying the amenities the plantation had to offer.

Upon opening the door to the rental unit, we were overtaken by a musty smell, plus the place was a mess. There were torn carpets, dirty pans in the sink, and the beds were a mess. This wasn't our idea how to spend Thanksgiving weekend, let alone a night. I wondered to myself if this place was reserved just for Yankees.

I immediately returned to the rental office and described the current condition of the unit to the agent at the desk. In typical, old-fashioned, southern style hospitality, he apologized and immediately offered us another unit, one that was more expensive than the one we had rented, but for the same price. After checking it out to make sure we weren't being snookered, we took it. The unit was larger than the first, had three bedrooms rather than two, and was well furnished.

After settling in, we had dinner at a local Cracker Barrel restaurant not too far from our accommodations. Cracker Barrels were the closest things we found to diners in the south. Over the next three days we enjoyed several good meals at nearby The Crazy Crab restaurant, went horseback riding, and took advantage of the many unique shops in the area. We even put our feet in the ocean. Having enjoyed our stay, we made plans to do it again the following year.

Stuck in the South

After being employed by NCR for about 18 months, I was laid off from my job. Their computer business tanked, and it was a "last in first to go" situation. The company layoff compensation plan included 2 weeks salary and a $30 phone card. Also, the unemployment benefits in South Carolina were meager compared to northern states. It was only a few hundred dollars a week. This was not much compared to the salary I had been earning, let alone paying the mortgage.

Not being in a position to readily move back north to Jersey, as my daughter was in her senior year at Dutch Fork High School, I started searching for work to pay the bills. At that time there were no websites like Indeed, Career Builder, or Zip Recruiter. So, I used every tool available to me including old fashioned newspaper ads, networking, and phone books in my quest.

My search for jobs in the Sunday paper, The State, yielded few results. There was one job as a reporter for the city newspaper, but it didn't pay much. And I never really enjoyed my experience in that position years earlier. Another advertisement I remember from the paper was for a cemetery closer. In my mind I could imagine it as a job putting the final cover on a grave. I never applied for that one.

Networking and cold calling turned out to be my best options. During my time at NCR, I had joined a local film association and made several connections that proved valuable after my layoff.

At a local trade show in Columbia, I met two men, Mitch Smith, the main salesman and a graduate of The Citadel, and Steve Lounsberry, a man with an idea for using computers to train employees. The two had just started a computer-based training company called Pinnacle East. They were chasing down a bunch of leads but didn't have an instructional designer who could develop the programs they were proposing.

We hit it off and I began developing scripts for them. The first project was a series of programs for Fleet Mortgage based in Columbia and with offices in Florence, SC. Over the next few months, I created several programs for Fleet, as well as Hardee's Food Systems, Hoechst Celanese, and a sample attendance program for BMW which had just opened a plant in Greenville, SC.

While writing for Pinnacle East, I contacted other companies. Taking advantage of connections I had made through networking and cold calls, I developed a safety video script for the Baptist Medical Center in Columbia. Working with a production house in Charleston, I wrote a hazard protocol video for Ryan's Family Steakhouses. I also drafted a video script for the South Carolina Retirement System, as well as a forklift training program for a PR company located in Florence, SC.

Law and Order in South Carolina

It's hard to turn on the TV and not find an episode of Law and Order playing on some channel. Whether or not you liked the program it is one of the longest running crime dramas on television. There are also many spin offs like Criminal Intent, Organized Crime, and Special Victims Unit. The first half of each program dealt with a crime, police procedures, and apprehending the bad guys before taking them to trial. I also had an opportunity to develop some programs on police procedures, not for a major studio but for South Carolina Educational Television.

As I mentioned earlier, I knocked on a lot of doors to find ways to make a living without resorting to a life of crime. However, in a way, crime did find me. One of those doors was to the South Carolina Criminal Justice Academy which worked with South Carolina Educational Television (SCETV) to develop training programs for police officers in the state. Through networking I learned that the Academy was always looking for writers to script videos on the proper procedures and skills for investigating and solving crimes.

From my journalism experience, I knew I could write a script on almost any subject if I could get answers to five basic questions: Who, What, When, Where, and Why. With a resume and samples of past projects, I met with Richard Shealy, the media supervisor at the Academy and an ETV producer. By the time the meeting ended I walked out with an assignment to script a video dealing with illegal narcotic distributors, which I called "Up the Ladder."

I developed the script for the segment by interviewing several experienced narcotics officers. They provided me with the procedures for uncovering the identities of top drug dealers by properly interrogating low-level street sellers. Once the script was approved, I attended the filming of the program on site. After it was edited, the program was approved by the Academy and became part of their training library.

Based on the Academy's satisfaction with my first script, I was offered a second. This segment dealt with the proper procedures for safely approaching suspicious vehicles. It was built on the fact that if you didn't do this correctly you could easily end up dead. I titled it "Right or Dead Wrong." This segment also became part of the Academy's library.

That was the final program I wrote for the Academy and SCETV. Upon its completion I packed my carpetbags and prepared to move back to New Jersey to restart my life in Yankee land.

Planes, Planes, and Automobiles

I never was a great traveler, especially by plane. When it comes to boats, forget it. One of my first plane experiences as an adult ended up with me a bright shade of green by the time we landed. However, as I traveled more and more by plane, for business and vacations, the more I got used to it. Most of the time it was one plane ride to a place and then a return trip a few days later. No big deal.

Even though I had picked up freelance work in the Columbia area I was looking for a steadier gig. I traveled to different locations around the country for job interviews. Then a chat or discussion on the phone. If you passed the first round, you boarded a plane and went. In this case, I was able to schedule interviews with two different companies in the northeast on one trip. However, it meant six planes in two days, something of a record for me.

The trip started early in the morning from Columbia, SC. My wife dropped me off at the Columbia airport. It was pretty small. You could actually drive right up to the main building, park for a few dollars a day, and walk directly into the terminal. There were few direct flights to anywhere from Columbia. In most cases you had to connect through Charlotte or Pittsburgh to get to your destination.

On this particular day, the first leg of my journey took me to Pittsburgh, PA, for a connection to Long Island. Luckily, my connecting flight was on time. Without too long of a layover I flew to Long Island for my first meeting. It was an interview with Arrow Electronics for a technical training position. Upon landing, I rented a car and following directions, I drove out the Long Island Expressway to Arrow for an afternoon interview with the hiring manager. We had a good discussion and I learned in detail what they were looking for. I didn't think it was the right job for me. Neither did the manager.

Undaunted, but not disgusted, I drove back to the airport, returned the car, and waited for my next connection to Boston. Crazy as it might seem, I flew to Boston for a connection to Newark. At the Newark airport, there was a chauffeur waiting for me. He drove me to a nearby Hilton where I stayed overnight. The next morning I had an interview with Mercedes Benz. After the interview I was driven back to Newark where I caught a return flight to Pittsburgh. And from Pittsburgh back to Columbia. I was becoming an experienced traveler. No job offers but a lot of air miles.

Meet Me in St. Louis

Early in 1996, as part of my job search, I sent out resumes everywhere east of the Mississippi. One day I was contacted by a head-hunting company about doing training design work in St. Louis, MO., for Metal Container Corp., a division of Anheuser-Busch Brewing Company.

After a phone interview, I flew to St. Louis from Columbia and interviewed in person with a lady named Karen Brown, the project manager, for the job. I ended up with the gig. Being a casual dress kind of guy, the one problem for me was the dress code. I had to wear a white shirt and tie every day. However, the job paid $50.00 an hour. I figured at 40 hours it would amount to $2000 per week. It was worth the sacrifice. The company was somewhat flexible about the hours, so I made arrangements to work five days one week and four days the next. This way I could fly home every other week for a long weekend to spend time with my family.

With the help of the head-hunter, I was able to rent an apartment just outside of St. Louis. From there I could take the light rail system into the office every day. I packed up my clothes and some essentials on a Saturday morning and drove to St. Louis from Columbia with a one-night stay at a motel in Paducah, Kentucky. I arrived the next day at the apartment. I checked in at the rental office and then went to the apartment. It was furnished, except for bed sheets, which I had brought from home. After a quick survey of what was lacking, I found a Target nearby and made a few purchases to meet my needs. I also found a Save-A-Lot supermarket close by where I could shop for food.

The next day I decided to drive into St. Louis and park near the office. I walked in the building at 9:00 am in the morning, met up with Karen Brown and was introduced to her team. It wasn't tremendously creative work, but it paid the bills.

After a month in the apartment outside the city, I decided to move to a high-rise in downtown St. Louis. This was a necessity as I was on the first floor of a two-story apartment complex and every night the resident above would take a shower at 3:30 in the morning, like clockwork, and keep me awake until sunrise.

The office for this training group was on the second floor in a large downtown building. It shared space with J.B. White, a major department store several floors above. In the beginning of this experience, I worked in a cubicle and had a desktop computer. The training group was under the guise of well-known consulting company. However, I doubted the training experience and knowledge of the people in charge. They believed in a total lack of privacy, had most workers seated in a line, so they could be observed by the supervisors at all times. They also frowned on interaction and the sharing of ideas.

After work, for exercise, I would often jog around the St. Louis Arch, as it was only a block from the apartment. On my jog I also discovered a floating McDonalds restaurant the only one I had ever seen. If I didn't feel like cooking for dinner, I'd call around to several Red Lobsters in the area to see which was serving flounder, one of the only seafoods I eat. If I felt like a real burger, I'd head out to Blueberry Hill for a good one.

Though I didn't care much for the work, I considered staying in the St. Louis area and even looked for places where my wife and I could live. There were sections of the town that reminded me very much of Philly. However, those plans came to an end when I was un-ceremonially dismissed from the job.

The Long Drive Home

After five months into the job with Metal Container, my position was terminated while I was away for a weekend visit with my family in New Jersey. That Friday afternoon I received a call from a co-worker, Susan Wilkens, telling me what had occurred during a staff meeting with the training group earlier that day.

The manager didn't have the balls to tell me face-to-face before I left. After receiving the call, I phoned my brother and sister, both attorneys to consider my next steps. They told me to remain cool and they would see what they could do. In the meantime, I planned my return trip which was to take place that Sunday evening based on the advanced airline tickets I had purchased.

On Sunday evening my wife dropped me off at the Atlantic City airport where I was supposed to take a short flight to Newark, NJ and then fly directly from Newark to St Louis. As it turned out the flight from Atlantic City was delayed. By the time we landed in Newark, I had missed my scheduled flight to St. Louis. As luck would have it, I was able to schedule a later flight. However, by the time I arrived in St. Louis, the light rail service had stopped for the night, and there were no cabs available. This was before anyone thought about Uber or Lyft.

Not wanting to stay at the airport all night, I managed to get on a shuttle taking the flight crew to a hotel near my apartment. They dropped me off several blocks from my place and I gave the driver a nice tip for taking me close to my final destination. I safely reached my apartment a few minutes later and tried to sleep, knowing that I had a long day ahead of me.

I awoke at about 5:30 am on that Monday morning, showered, and ate a light breakfast. I then walked the few blocks to the building where I had been employed. I let myself into the office with my key and located my personal belongings. They were next to the desk where I had worked. As some of my former coworkers arrived, I said my goodbyes and wished them well. I also turned in my office key to another manager, as the one who fired me was nowhere to be seen.

I then returned to my downtown apartment and made arrangements for my rented furniture to be picked up and for turning off my cable and phone service. Next, I went to the rental office, explained the situation, and canceled my lease. The rental agent was very understanding and didn't give me any problems. I then turned to the task of packing all my belongings including the plates, pots and pans, and my small television. Once that was completed, I took one last walk around the Arch, had a light supper, and tried to sleep.

The next morning, my last in St. Louis, I woke up early, and was able to pack the car with several trips to the parking garage under the building. It was about 6:00 am when I finally started my journey back to New Jersey. I drove across the Mississippi and headed east through Indiana along route 70. It was a dull drive, mile after mile of flatlands.

By about 1:00 pm I reached the Ohio border, and headed toward Columbus, where my sister had her law office. By about 2:00 pm I managed to find her place, parked, and walked in. She greeted me and off we went to lunch at a nearby restaurant. I explained the situation to her in detail, and then headed out once again for our shore home in Ocean City, New Jersey.

My original plan was to stop in Harrisburg, PA for the night and then travel to Ocean City the next day. I ended up in Harrisburg at about 9:00 pm. "Hmm," I thought to myself, "I'm only about three hours from home, why not just go." With an apple and a bag of chocolate cookies, I pushed on. Long story short, I reached Ocean City at about 12:30 am that night. I had arrived safely, but I was completely exhausted and wiped out for the next three days.

The Yankees Retreat

Unlike General Sherman who marched his way through Georgia during the Civil War, we decided to permanently retreat North after three years in the South. When we first moved to Columbia in 1993, NCR paid for the moving company to pack up our belongings and furniture and transport them and one of our cars to our newly purchased home in Lexington County just outside of Columbia.

A year after I was laid off and when my daughter, Laura, graduated from Dutch Fork High School, we decided to move back to New Jersey. By the way, she graduated number 2 in her class. She would have been number one except for the fact that she was a Yankee.

On our retreat from the South we were paying for the transport of our possessions back to Jersey. As a result we were a great deal more selective of what we were bringing back. We put out a lot of things in the trash including books, clothing, magazines, and furniture we weren't crazy about.

Since our new townhouse in Delran, New Jersey wasn't finished on time, we made arrangements with the moving company to put our furniture in storage for a few weeks. This go-round, we packed ourselves. However, when the moving crew arrived, it was a very unprofessional group. It seemed like they had just hired these folks off the street, gave them company shirts, but little knowledge about moving and loading furniture. They scratched the floors, rolled boxes down the steps from the second floor, damaged furniture, and pieces went missing.

When our possessions were finally delivered to New Jersey several weeks later, the moving company ended up paying for a lot of repairs and replacements. I guess the Confederates finally got their revenge on us Yankees.

Chapter 6: Ocean City Classics

Ocean City, New Jersey promotes itself as "America's Greatest Family Resort." Summering and then living in the town on a full-time basis I learned a good deal about its history, people, and politics. It's a dry town, but you never know it from the empty beer cans and liquor bottles on trash day. Still, it's an interesting place to live. Of course, I like it best 9 months of the year: September - May. What follows are some of my observations of this shore town and the people who inhabit it.

Haunting Memories of Ocean City Dining

When we first started to summer in Ocean City during the late 1970's, we sampled several restaurants. These visits were based on advertisements in the local papers like the Sentinel and Gazette, and on the radio, as well as suggestions from friends. One place we kept hearing about on the radio was Bookers. It used to stand at Eighth Street and Central Avenue. The portions were small, the prices high, and the vegetables canned. It was a typical tourist trap. Based on our experience it was a "one and done" adventure.

Near where we were renting during the summer months were several take-out restaurants that earned our business. There was Campbells on Asbury Avenue near 33rd street. My daughter liked the meatballs of all things to eat at a place that specialized in seafood. Our favorite for many years was Hickman's Seafood at 12th and Asbury. Their prices were reasonable, and the portions were fair. Both places have been gone for years. Campbells was sold and the lots became several duplexes. Hickman's space became part of Benny's which now sells bread and prepared foods.

The original Benny's was an OC classic and only sold bread and rolls. It was a small store front with a wooden screen door. The owner didn't open the wooden screen door until exactly 9:00 am, no matter how many people were lined up outside. It was like Seinfeld's "Soup Nazi," only with bread. At 9:00 am the door was unlocked, and the customers filed in, one by one, in line, and ordered their bread or rolls, paid for their purchases and filed out.

Another place I remember was Mick and Beans, on the corner of 18th and Asbury. It was famous for crabs. You could smell them a block away. When the restaurant closed, it was replaced by condos. For several years after, I swear you could still smell the crabs when you walked by.

My late friend Rich Loveland, always liked to go to Shafto's, a small eatery on Asbury that is also only a memory. Rich liked the turkey and trimmings.

If you were in the mood for ice cream or a sundae on a hot summer's evening, there was the Dairy Queen on 34th Street. It too is gone, replaced by a bank offering cold hard cash.

The Highest Bidder

Most of our time on the beach in Ocean City is spent on 37th Street. We have been going to that beach for over forty years. During that stretch we made many friends. Most were older than us. However, it was almost like a family. A few folks worth mentioning include Bill and Pat Todd, from McLean, Virginia. They had a summer house on Asbury Avenue. There was also John and Doris Kemper, from Delaware County, PA. John was a retired nuclear engineer and Doris a former nurse. Their summer home was on Haven Avenue. One other couple of note was Rich and Lori Loveland. Rich owned an insurance agency in Bridgeton, NJ. He married Lori, after his first wife, Mary Sue, passed. They had a condo at Bluewater, a condo development next to the 34th street bridge.

These were couples who liked to spend time on the beach and in the ocean. As they got older and would go in for a swim, I would play lifeguard. While they were in the water, I often wondered what I would do if more than one got in trouble at the same time, "Who would I save first?" I jokingly said to them, "I'll save the person who offers me the most money first."

That winter, I received a handwritten Christmas card from Rich Loveland. Attached to the card was a twenty-dollar bill. On the card was written, "Save me first."

Opening Night Tradition

If you're an Ocean City local there's only one place to be on the island that third Thursday of the month in March. That place is opening day at Kessel's Corner, an old-fashioned, family friendly restaurant and ice cream parlor located at 28th and Asbury. In advance of the opening date, folks drive by the closed establishment every week looking for a sign announcing the exact opening date.

When that Thursday arrives, you'd think it was the grand opening of a new five-star eatery. But you would be wrong. Many a family is lined up outside or trying to squeeze in the front door waiting for an empty booth or table. On opening day, Kessel's regulars come from all over to be there for that Thursday. They pour in from Cherry Hill, Philly, Bucks, Montgomery, and Delaware Counties. By the crowds you'd think it was the middle of the summer season. But you would be wrong. It's a tradition, one we have been part of for decades.

Walking in on opening day and almost every day, customers see Dave Young, the owner, wearing a baseball cap and an apron. He's hard at work on the grill flipping burgers for Kessel Specials, assembling wraps, or checking orders to make sure everything is right. He could also be mixing his famous beef vegetable soup which is only served weekdays during the spring and fall seasons. If he knows you or your face, you'll always get a smile and a hello, and then it's back to work.

The red cushioned booths are all clean and shiny along with the straight tables in the center of the room. The black and white tile floor is spanking clean, ready for the customer onslaught about to begin. On the wall above the row of booths, Coke collectables and model trains fill the shelf. You'll also find pictures of Dave's family on the walls. It's on that day that the season really begins, not Memorial Day.

Repair Rather than Replace

How many times have you had an appliance die or break and you would like it replaced? It could be a refrigerator, a dryer, or some other appliance. You call the manufacturer or warranty company and they will often tell you their policy is to repair rather than replace.

Before we purchased our first home in Ocean City we rented different places for several years at the south end of the island near 37th street. One of the locations we inhabited for several summers was on Central Avenue, a few houses in from 37th Street. It was an older home owned by the Knauer family which even has a town named after them, Knauerville, in northeastern Pennsylvania. Dave Knauer, the property owner, was an accomplished businessman who had built numerous industrial parks and hotels in Pennsylvania. His family lived above us during the summer months on this property on Central Avenue, just one block from the beach.

Dave was a stocky fellow who loved to laugh. He even occasionally played beach volleyball with us across the alley on a small court owned by the Winther family. Based on his style of play, Dave had gained a nickname, "The Claw," from how he often hit the ball with his large hands.

Dave loved to putter around the property and repair things rather than replace them. On one occasion, my daughter, Laura, who was just seven at the time, noticed the wooden toilet seat in one of the bathrooms in our first-floor rental apartment was chipped. She didn't want to sit on it – afraid of splinters on her tush, I guess. We asked Dave to replace the toilet seat which Lincoln might have sat on during the Civil War.

One Saturday morning, Dave came down the steps from upstairs with several sheets of fine sandpaper, a can of white paint, and a one-inch paint brush. He went into the bathroom and did his thing – sanding the seat and putting a fresh coat of white paint on it. He then stood up, looked proudly at his accomplishment, and remarked, "Don't sit on it for a few hours." Then he left with a broad smile on his face.

Apparently, Dave believed in repairing rather than replacing almost everything, even down to toilet seats. He must have read the story about how many thousands of dollars toilet seats cost the government years ago. I often wondered if he followed the same process at his hotels and industrial parks. That must have kept him busy. However, we were not privy to all his habits.

Long Distance Turnoff

Almost everyone has heard the joke in some form or another of how many people of one ethnicity or another it takes to change a light bulb or what happens when you pass a message down the line from one person to another and another and see how it has changed by the time it reaches its ultimate destination. We had a similar situation, but it involved turning off the water to the outside showers in our first home in Ocean City on 37th Street.

We purchased our first Ocean City property in 1989. It was a second-floor, three-bedroom condo at 37th and West Avenue in the south end. We handled all the maintenance and care of the building for both floors. Each year, with the coming of winter, we would turn off the water to the outside showers to prevent the pipes from freezing. The turnoff valves were located in the crawl space under the building. To reach them required crawling several feet on your stomach. Once there you had to put a wrench on them to loosen the valves and let the water drain. It was critical to turn the valves in the right direction without stripping the grooves. I performed the task myself faithfully from 1989 through 1992.

When the time came to turn off the water after the summer of 1993, I was in Columbia, South Carolina, and the task was left to my two sons, Stephen and Dennis, and their significant others. They called me one weekend and asked for instructions to do the job. This is where the fun began, as neither are mechanically inclined. There was a winding line of communication from South Carolina to South Jersey from the top floor of the condo, where the phone was located, down 2 flights of steps to the garage, and ultimately to the crawl space where one of my sons was located. What should have been a 5-minute job turned into a 45-minute exercise of should I do this, or should I do that? Which way should I turn the wrench? It seemed like an Abbott and Costello skit similar to "Who's on First?"

Eventually they got it right and for the next few years until I returned from my adventure in South Carolina it was accomplished without a long-distance call.

Chicken Delight

For many years when we wanted chicken for dinner, we would order broasted chicken breasts from Hickman's seafood on Asbury Avenue. The breasts were always plump, tasty, fresh, and juicy. When Hickman's closed we were forced to find an alternative source.

With KFC a good distance away, and off the island, our closest substitute was Acme brand fried chicken only a few blocks away at 34th street. Acme had pretty good chicken, either whole or pieces and at a reasonable price. They also sold Mr. Ron's Cole Slaw, considered by my wife to be the best.

Late one afternoon, wanting to have chicken for dinner, I went to the Acme and asked the counter person in the deli section for four nice breasts. She was standing next to an older lady also behind the counter, and without missing a beat replied, "Between the two of us we have four nice breasts." As a person with usually a quick response, I stood there stunned. I had no reply. I just stood there in amazement and smiled.

The Jews of Ocean City

When we first arrived in Ocean City more than 40 years ago, I had a feeling there weren't many Jewish people in this town. There were no synagogues, no kosher delicatessens, and no one to play Jewish geography with. If I wanted a synagogue, I learned, there was one in Wildwood, and several others in Northfield and Margate, including a Jewish Community Center. If I wanted Jews and deli's, I guess I should have moved to Margate, Ventnor, or Lantic City, but my wife loved "America's Greatest Family Resort," as the town bills itself.

A Jewish deli tried to make it in Ocean City several years ago at Ninth and Central. While it was there, I enjoyed great brisket sandwiches, and the corned beef was out of this world. Real stuff. The owner moved on but tried to franchise the business. However, the new operator cut back on the original concept and it didn't last. The place didn't even smell the same: an important ingredient for a successful kosher restaurant. It was replaced by a typical shore café.

As for the Jews in Ocean City, at one time I thought there were only three. One was my friend Bernie, with whom I played volleyball. He lived a few houses from us on West Avenue. I knew he was Jewish because I went to high school with his sister, Ruthi, and she was Jewish. The only other Jewish person I knew in town was Robert, a partner in Boyer's Market on Asbury Avenue. Robert at one time refereed games between the Harlem Globetrotters and The Washington Generals. He moved to Florida, the Jewish waiting room, and has since passed, so one-third of the Jewish population is gone. I wonder what the next census will reveal.

The Artist on 11th Street

When we purchased our first home in Ocean City in 1989, the original owner, who built the property in 1964, lived downstairs on a rental basis. She had sold the building to the Morrissey brothers, after her husband had passed. The building at that time had faded green siding on the exterior which we felt needed an upgrade.

As it turned out, the Morrissey brothers were willing to let us handle the maintenance of the building. As long as we apprised them of what we were planning to do and obtained several bids on projects, they went along with us and split the cost down the middle.

Our first undertaking was to replace the faded siding with something different. There was a new color that had just come out, coral bisque. We felt it would make our home stand out from the others in the area, which were mostly gray. As requested by the other owners, we got several quotes for the job. With their approval we had the old siding removed and the new color siding installed by a local contractor.

The rear wall of the property, where the garage was located, faced the alley between West Avenue and Asbury. It was bare and blank. Having returned from a business trip in Florida with a shirt for my wife showing a seascape, we got the idea to put a seascape on the bare back wall.

During our travels into downtown we had noticed a storefront at the corner of Asbury and 11th street with seashore artwork for sale. The colorful and whimsical artwork, made of scrap wood, caught our attention. The store was owned by an artist who went by the name of Gar and his pieces were adorning a number of houses around the island. You can still see many of these original works of art today. There's even one mounted on a house on the left side of the street when you come into Ocean City over the Ninth Street Bridge.

We went in and met Gar. He was a short fellow about five feet six with long white hair and a beard. We brought along the seascape shirt I had purchased in Florida to explain our idea. He was interested in doing the project and offered to sketch out a design for our back wall aquarium.

Within a week, Gar had created a design with a variety of sea life including sharks, turtles, angelfish, and barracudas, along with aquatic plants at the base. With some minor suggestions, we approved his sketch. Two weeks later he was back with the finished pieces, a ladder, and some screws to attach the pieces to the wall. The end result was a unique and attractive addition to our home. In fact, many people drove by the alley just to see this colorful aquatic scene.

We were so pleased with Gar's work that we hired him to create a custom, seashore-styled wooden Indian for us to stand in our entranceway. When we moved to a year-round house in the city several years later, we had him make a lighthouse address sign for the front of our new home and a colorful seagull to adorn the rear above the garage. We also purchased several other pieces of Gar's artwork that caught our eye as we passed his shop. Every year at Thanksgiving we put out his pilgrim and turkey, and at Christmas his angel and snowman appear.

Gar left us several years ago, but his artwork on so many houses remain as a testament to a creative man who enjoyed what he was doing.

Handyman Jack

I remember with a smile a one-person show on Broadway by the late comedian Jackie Mason, "The World According to Me." As part of his performance Jackie discussed how many folks associate Jewish people with being doctors, dentists, lawyers, or accountants, especially the proud parents of these professionals. "My son is a doctor." "My daughter is a lawyer at a prestigious firm in the city." Even if the offspring is a truck driver, the proud parent claims the child is a controller in a trucking company.

Not everyone is born to be a physician or an engineer. There are many professions needed in today's modern world. Take for instance a handyman. Finding a good and reliable handyman is tough. When you can't do a repair around the house yourself, and realize it, you need to call someone you can trust to do the job, when you need it done, and at a fair price.

Today you can find handymen online through Home Advisor, Angi, business cards displayed at the hardware store or listed in the local paper. However, it's often trial and error to find a good and reliable one. In our case, a referral from a satisfied friend was a great way to go. We found our handyman, Jack, through a conversation with a friend in the locker room at the Ocean City Aquatic and Fitness Center. I was commenting on some work we needed done and a friend, Bill, who had been in town for years recommended a fellow named Jack Breslau.

We called Jack and he answered the phone. We explained what we needed done. Jack told us when he would be available to look at the job and give us a price. This was over ten years ago, and we still call on Jack when we need him. We also recommend him to other friends.

When you reach Jack by phone, he will almost always pick up. If you leave your name and number, on the off chance he can't answer, he'll call you back to make an appointment to look at the job. He'll even call you when he's on his way to tell you he'll be there on time or a little late. Jack always looks at the job and if he can't handle it himself, he'll recommend someone who can.

The Pool People

When we first moved to Ocean City full-time, we discovered the Ocean City Aquatic and Fitness Center at 18th street. Membership was the best bargain in the whole town. My wife enjoyed the water exercise classes given daily in the shallow end of the Olympic-sized swimming pool by a variety of different instructors. My wife also had a nickname for each, like Mary Sunshine and Poster Girl who taped colorful instructions to the front wall for her students to follow. Attendance for each of the sessions varied by how the participants liked the instructors. During the summer season there were often 50 or more taking a class at the same time.

While my wife was aqua exercising in the shallow end, I played deep water volleyball at the other end near the diving board, where the water is 13-feet deep. Here I was introduced to an entirely new cast of friends and characters I call "the pool people." The number of volleyball players varied from a few during the winter to sometimes more than 20 during the busy summer season.

The anointed leader and co-founder of the original group of players was a gracious lady named Helen Newsome. Helen brought the balls and kept the peace during the game. Sadly,

Helen died too soon from pancreatic cancer and is sorely missed. Another memorable player I met early on was Mary Anthony, a single woman with a short temper who hardly ever smiled. There was also Peg Lamb, who played with us into her nineties. Peg often brought family to the game during the summer. She loved to keep count and see how many times we could get the ball over the net before it hit the water. Other players who came for years included Connie Stack, a former nurse. She would come three times a week from Margate to play. We often joked that Connie didn't need a floatation belt as her body structure was well-proportioned to keep her afloat.

The players varied in age and original occupations. There was Marianna K, whose family owns Dino's Diner in Seaville, NJ. Early on, folks thought we were married because we left the pool at the same time. Marianna would also organize a pool luncheon at her family's restaurant twice a year; one at the end of summer and a second at Christmas time.

Many of the regular v-ball players had nicknames, like Barbara and Mike Crowley from Sea Isle City. We fondly referred to them as The Queen and the Prince. Barbara even told us her friends once gave her a coronation (enough said). There was playful Walt Sudol, the splasher king, a Vietnam vet who suffered from the effects of that conflict. Other players included Big Joe, Wetsuit Jack, and Al Reeves, a former prison guard and dog lover whom we called Big Al in reference to a character from the TV show Laugh-In.

There was also Roger and Kate White. They met on a small sailing ship cruise. Roger, from Wales, was a member of the crew and Kate was a passenger. In addition, there was Little Pat and Big Pat. Little Pat, a former schoolteacher, loved talking football and cars. Her football comments often appeared in the Atlantic City Press after an Eagles game, win or lose.

Due to COVID-19, the pool was closed for several months as a safety precaution. When the town partially reopened the pool there were no formal water classes or volleyball. You had to sign up each day for a time slot with a limited number of participants in the pool at any one time. We signed up to go every day, five days a week at 10:00 in the morning.

During our sessions we made friends with several other people, including Bonnie Miles, who loved buying things on Amazon, Kathy K, who only cooked gluten-free, and Dave Jungblut, a dedicated environmentalist and astronomy instructor at Atlantic Cape Community College.

When the pool reopened on a limited basis we were permitted to swim/exercise for 45 minutes and then required to exit in order for the lifeguards to clean the area for the next group. The head lifeguard was named Lynn. I had known her for several years and she knew the pool inside and out. She also sat near my family on the beach in the summertime.

Lynn made sure folks social-distanced at the pool and would blow her whistle when there were five minutes remaining in your time slot. I often joked that if she swallowed her whistle, she would still manage to tweet so everyone could hear.

Good Neighbor Steve

Like Good Neighbor Sam, played by Jack Lemon, in the 1964 film by the same name, my next-door neighbor Steve Carchedi will do almost anything to help you out.

When we first moved to Ocean City on a full-time basis, we had nice neighbors on both sides. To the left was the Neplasic family, Jim and Sharon, and their two sons, Jimmy and Owen. Jim was into banking while Sharon taught in the Ocean City Public School System. The neighbors on the right were an older couple, the Orios. They lived in the Swarthmore area and spent many of their summers in Ocean City.

Eventually, the Orios sold their rancher to a local builder who had recently purchased the lot on the other side of them. The Orios got an excellent price for their property, considering the builder wanted it badly. On the two lots the builder constructed a McMansion for the mayor of Ocean City, a good friend of his. The home had a large, modern kitchen, game room, a winding staircase to the second floor, and loads of amenities. A few years later, the mayor put his house up for sale. After some time on the market, he eventually sold it to Steve and Caroline, a couple from Lower

Gwynedd, PA. They, along with their two sons, Max and Cole, are true good neighbors.

Steve is one handy guy. He has almost every tool you could imagine including a wide array of gizmos, saws and wrenches. Plus, he loves to putter and come up with projects to complete around his house. Almost no job is too much for Steve to tackle and he is always ready to give you a helping hand or a suggestion on a neighbor's project, from straightening doors or rebuilding an outside shower base, to reinforcing frames.

There is practically no limit to Steve's skills. He constructed a large cage around his air conditioning units to lessen the noise. He refinished the mahogany flooring on his front porch himself. He and Caroline have made their property a showplace.

If he sees you considering a project, Steve will make a suggestion to improve the design and then give you a helping hand completing it. You don't have to be his next-door neighbor to receive Steve's assistance. Neighbors up and down the alley are recipients of Steve's knowledge, skills, and tools.

Appreciating his help, I often offer my assistance as a laborer or provide him with gardening knowledge or produce from my garden as small repayment.

Blueberry Bill

My wife loves frozen blueberries with her Cheerios in the morning. Frozen berries help to chill the milk. They are also a great source of antioxidants. For many years, when the local supermarket offered eight pints for sale at a special price, we would purchase the pints, flash freeze them, and then place the frozen berries in plastic bags and keep them in the freezer until needed.

When a friend, Bill Todd, told us where we could purchase large frozen berries directly from a nearby farm at a great price, we jumped at the chance. The farm turned out to be The American Blueberry Company just outside of Hammonton, NJ, a small town that calls itself "The Blueberry Capital of the World." With Bill's directions and a map, I eventually found the facility. It offered frozen berries year-round and fresh ones when in season.

For several years, every few months I would stop at American Blueberry on Route 559 and purchase a ten-pound box of the frozen berries. As the COVID-19 pandemic came to an end, and being in need of a supply of these frozen antioxidants, I checked out the company online to see if they had berries available. Apparently, they no longer sold the frozen berries. Undaunted, I began a search for a new source.

I figured there must be other farms around Hammonton selling these valuable antioxidants. An online search turned up the name Blueberry Bill's Farm, also in Hammonton proper. I picked up the phone and called the number listed on their website. It rang and rang. No one picked up. A few minutes after hanging up, my phone rang. It was Blueberry Bill calling back. In a friendly farmer tone, he told me he had frozen blueberries and they were about the same price I had paid at the American Blueberry Company. I told him I'd be up in the area in a few days to pick up ten pounds.

On my next trip to Hammonton, I found the place without much trouble, which for me, a fly-by- the-seat-of-my-pants guy, was amazing. I pulled up in front of the warehouse and parked. I entered the building looking for Blueberry Bill, but no one was around. I walked outside and noticed a couple of workers tending some crops. I called to them. However, they apparently didn't understand English. After a few minutes I went back to the car and called Bill's number. He answered and said he would send someone to the warehouse to help me.

Within a few minutes, the warehouse foreman pulled up. I explained that I wanted ten pounds of blueberries. He went over to one of the freezers in the building and pulled out a 50-pound box. He opened the box and after putting an empty container on a scale began pouring these large, beautiful berries into a smaller box. After reaching 10 pounds, he stopped and closed the container. I handed him 20 dollars and said, "Thank you."

A few months later, when we needed to replenish our supply, I brought my wife with me as we were also going to stop at Bagliani's market in Hammonton. As we approached Hammonton, I had my wife call Blueberry Bill, just to make sure someone was there this time. Bill answered and gave us different instructions. He told us to pull up to the warehouse and go inside to the second freezer on the right. There were 10-pound boxes in that freezer. He said to take one box and leave the money in the freezer. We did. That's what I call cold, hard cash and it was worth every penny.

Number 44

When it is time for a holiday dinner, like at Easter, Thanksgiving, or Christmas, our children and grandchildren flock to the family homestead in Ocean City to celebrate and feast. For Easter it's usually ham and turkey. At Thanksgiving it's turkey and chicken with all the trimmings. Not everyone likes turkey. At Christmas it's ricotta-filled crepes, a filet mignon roast and twice baked potatoes. Almost everyone likes everything for that meal.

When it's time to clear the table after gorging themselves on the feast, and before dessert is even considered, a crowd starts making its way into the kitchen with their empty plates until my wife or I yell, "Number 44," which stops the tribe in their tracks.

Number 44 has a special meaning to our clan. If you ever saw the GEICO commercial with former football player Ickey Woods, a former NFL fullback with Cincinnati Bengals, standing in a deli line waiting to be served, you get the idea. Wait until your turn. We can only fit so many people in the kitchen at one time. Of course, few are able to do his famous "Ickey shuffle" once allowed in.

Screens, Screams, and Saints

Our home in Ocean City has 24 windows. Many of them are located on the first floor, including several in the garage. However, seven of them are on the second floor spread out over four bedrooms. Each window has a screen which we remove, wash, and dry before storing them away for the winter. Around Memorial Day we put them back in. This process has allowed the screens to survive over twenty years at the seashore with its salty air and natural corrosion.

Removing the screens are no problem, even in tight spaces. You just open the window, raise the sash, release the side tabs that hold the screen in place, and slide it into the room. Presto!

The difficulty is reinstalling those seven screens each year. To accomplish this task, I first move the drapes out of the way, raise the blinds, then unlock, and raise the window. Next, I get down on my knees, tilt the screen through the window and try and position it in the top track, and evenly on the sides. During this process, which is never successful on the first or second try, my family hears a lot of unintelligible words, and the names of several saints, even though I'm Jewish.

However, I think the saints have heard my cries and taken pity on me. Watching an episode of Shark Tank, I saw a product that could prevent my screams and keep my language civil and might allow me to get into heaven. There, on the show, was a flexible screen that bends, making it easier to install. I've ordered seven of these puppies for the second floor. Hopefully, they'll solve my problem and stop my yearly screams.

Sh*t always happens after 5 pm on a Friday Night

How many times has this happened to you? Something goes wrong with an appliance, your computer, email, or a toilet after 5 pm on a Friday night when most if not all repairmen have left for the day or don't answer their phones. Such an event happened to us. It was, of course, a Friday night after 5 pm on a hot summer day.

My wife had just walked into the garage and noticed water on the floor near the HVAC unit, and quickly called me to the scene. Water was coming out of the plastic pipe next to the air conditioning unit, flowing down the platform, and onto the floor. The boxes near the unit were soaked through on the bottom. A quick examination of the scene revealed that water was not freely exiting the AC unit's outside drainpipe and backing up into the garage.

Although water was slowly dripping from the drainpipe, it seems there was a blockage somewhere between the AC unit and the drain. As a result, water was pouring out of the overflow pipe in the garage.

We quickly turned off the AC and began the cleanup. Since it was after 5 pm we had little hope of reaching our regular HVAC repair folks until Monday morning. I then remembered that my friend, Lenny, had a son-in-law, Tom, who was a plumber and lived nearby. I thought he might be able to help us in our time of need. We had called on Tom in the past for several jobs and he always was able to meet our needs.

I quickly located Tom's number from our personal phone book and placed a call. Tom sadly didn't answer. Instead, I reached his answering machine. With few options available to us, I left a detailed message explaining our situation and waited. There was no return call that night.

Early the next day, I got up and went to get my wife her usual Saturday morning favorite cappuccino drink at the local Wawa at 34th street. On my return, we received a call from Tom. He explained that he had been out with his family on Friday night but would come over shortly to see what he could do.

Tom pulled up in the back of the house about 15 minutes later and surveyed the situation. He wasn't sure what he could do but would try and clear the clog with his battery-powered Milwaukee wet/dry vacuum. Tom went to the outside drain and attached his device to the spout. Within two minutes he had sucked out a gallon full of cloudy water and waste materials.

To see if the drain was completely unclogged my wife turned on the AC unit. No water came out the overflow pipe, but a stream of water flowed freely through the outside drain. I paid Tom whatever he asked, considering it was a summer emergency and he showed up right away – something you can't always count on in our little town, especially during the summer.

I took a close look at Tom's vacuum and ordered the exact same model just in case the situation ever arose again. In fact, the vacuum came in handy a few months later when I was attempting to turn off the outside water and drain the pipes for the winter. I always like to be prepared.

Never Too Old to Learn

It's often been said that you're never too old to learn something new. The first year we bought our year-round home in Ocean City I had the plumber who did the original work on the house show me how to turn off and disconnect the water to the outside hoses and the small sink in the garage. This was done to prevent the pipes in the crawlspace from freezing and possibly breaking during the winter months. All he did was turn off the hot and cold valves under the sink in the kitchen and disconnect the hot and cold-water bonnets in the garage and let them drain. He also poured some antifreeze down the drain. This "show me" experience cost me $65.00. For the next 20 years I performed the service myself at no charge with only a little elbow grease. I also was able to reconnect the system in the spring, also at no charge.

Recently we replaced the small sink with a larger one as the 20-year-old was beginning to leak. When the plumber installed the new unit I was no longer able to reach the bonnets to disconnect them and drain the pipes. I asked our handy plumber friend, Tom, if he could come over and do the disconnect. He did and I placed several small buckets under the severed connections to allow the water to drain. The hot water pipe drained quickly and stopped. It hardly filled the bucket. However, water continued to flow out from the cold-water pipe and filling buckets. When it finally stopped the next day, I emptied the bucket confident we had reached the end of the flowing cold water. I was wrong! The next morning there was water all over the garage floor leaving quite a mess for us to clean up.

Determined to end the flow, I opened one of the outside hose lines and hooked up my Milwaukee vacuum to it. Then I turned on the juice. Two minutes later, I turned off the machine and walked into the garage. Water was no longer coming from the pipe. I had definitely blown out all the water in the line, but it was all over the floor. This turned out to be a real learning experience. Next year, when it's time to drain the pipes, I'll attach a hose to the disconnected cold-water pipe and run it to a bucket, so water ends up in there rather than all over the garage floor. Either that or I will just call the plumber.

The Best Laid Plans

Several years ago, as I moved into my seventies, I purchased an electric snow thrower. My wife felt I was getting too old to do a lot of heavy shoveling. She was afraid I'd have a heart attack. Long story, short, the first year we didn't have much snow. What we did have was ice for which the device wasn't much good. Over the next three years we had no measurable snowball, so I didn't even assemble the machine.

Then in the winter of 2022, our luck ran out. First, we had twelve inches, the next week we got four more and then another 16 inches from a pair of coastal storms. As the second nor-easter was roaring down on us, I readied the snow thrower for the task ahead by spraying the chute with

Pam to keep the exiting snow from clogging it and laying out a 100-foot extension cord next to the machine. I was ready.

When the storm finally ended, I went out front to clear the steps and walkway to the house as the drifts were too high for the snow thrower to handle. As I began the task good neighbor Steve, all bundled from head to toe, was coming down the sidewalk clearing a path with his gas-powered thrower starting at one end of his property to the end of ours. There was no need for me to use my thrower.

After clearing the front sidewalk and steps and taking a short rest break, I went to tackle the back driveway where our cars were parked and covered with mounds of snow. Good neighbor Steve had already moved some of the snow in the alley with his gas blower but was running out of gas.

Using a small bucket, I began clearing the snow off my car so I could back it up into the alley and clear the pad. In the meantime, my wife began cleaning off her car so she could do the same thing. My plan was to move the cars into the alley and then clear the snow on the pad with my electric thrower. Once we moved our cars back, I went and plugged in the electric device and hit the starter. Nothing happened. I couldn't believe it. I had just used the machine a week earlier and it ran fine. Undaunted, I unplugged the machine from the outlet on the right side of the garage and plugged it in on the left. However, I had the same result. The machine appeared dead.

The only thing left to do was clear the pad by hand. As my wife and I moved the mounds of snow, neighbor Steve came out and took the shovel from my wife and began to help me. We moved enough snow to get his gas -powered thrower in close to clear the pad. Then he ran out of gas. With as much snow moved as possible, Steve went home.

I then decided to see if I could determine what was wrong with my electric. I checked the plow. It turned by hand. I checked the cords and the connections. They were all fine. Then, as I walked to the back of the garage, I could see the GFI blinking. Could that be the culprit? I went over and reset the switch and the blinking light went out.

Next, I tested the two outlets I had tried to use earlier with a portable lightbulb setup. They both worked. Apparently the GFI had been tripped by a portable heater in the back bedroom. The outlet upstairs and those in the garage were all on the same circuit.

With an understanding of the problem and having reached a successful resolution, I plugged in the electric thrower and went to work clearing the remaining snow in the alley. As a result of helping us, Steve had run out of gas and was unable to finish his driveway. Not wanting to let a good deed go unrewarded, I took my now working electric over to Steve's and helped him clear his pad.

Houdini Reincarnated

Even though we live on an island, Ocean City is host to a wide range of animals. In addition to well-known visitors like possums, foxes, muskrats, rabbits, and an occasional beaver who lost his contract for constructing a McMansion, in the winter when the weather turns cold, we often have family of field mice taking up residency in our garage. I can usually deal with them in traditional ways with old-fashioned traps. However, it seems these little guys are getting smarter every year.

This past winter I first noticed their arrival (since they didn't go to the check-in desk or make an advanced reservation) when I saw trails of small, black droppings along the walls and lower shelves. My first reaction was to think, "They're here." And they usually travel in pairs: a male and a female. As a result, I immediately placed several snap traps on the floor in those areas, baited them with a little peanut butter, and waited for the results.

The next morning, I opened the door to the garage and checked the traps. They weren't sprung but the peanut butter bait was gone. I thought, "How did they manage that? Are these stealth rodents? "Did one hold the spring back while the other took the bait and then switched places?" Undaunted, I reapplied the bait, in larger quantities, and waited until the next day. Once again, the bait was gone, and the traps bare. No mice, no peanut butter. This required a change in plan. Instead of peanut butter I baited the traps with cheese. The next morning I saw mixed results. I had gotten one visitor, but the other trap had no cheese and no mouse. It seems one mouse was smarter than the other, a real escape artist. I couldn't tell if it was the male, the female, or Harry Houdini reincarnated.

Knowing there was still at least one visitor taking a winter vacation in our garage who wasn't frightened or deterred by traditional traps, I resorted to another device, the dreaded glue trap. I purchased a pack of glue traps at the hardware store and placed two on the floor near the location of the earlier traditional traps and baited it with peanut butter. I had read that mice were nocturnal, basically nearsighted and would allow their sense of smell to get them in trouble. In this case, caught in a glue trap.

The next morning a peek into the garage led to a new surprise. One of the traps was missing. I got down on my hands and knees to see if I could find it. I did. It was under the legs of a foldaway cot we stored in the garage, and it was turned over. The trap was there, but no mouse. This critter was good and smart. It seems the rodent was able to drag the trap over to an area where it could wedge itself free of the trap by losing only a little fur but not its life.

Not wanting to be outsmarted by this winter visitor, I resorted to a new approach. I purchased a larger glue trap and using Gorilla Tape, secured the trap to the garage floor. Houdini would have to be stronger than King Kong to escape this time.

With the dawn of a new day, I checked out the garage. There was our visitor stuck in the unmovable trap. Finally, an end to its Houdini-like escapades. I just hope he doesn't come back as a muskrat.

Taking a Redneck to Breakfast

One of the many characters I met playing pickleball in Upper Township, Cape May County, was a fellow named John Kopitsky. At first glance, John looked like a typical redneck. He had long hair, a beard, colorful tattoos on his arms, always wore a dew cap, drove a high-wheeled jeep, owned a motorhome and a motorcycle, and hated Democrats. During the Trump presidency his fearless leader could do no wrong. Becoming friends with John was truly a learning experience.

When we played pickleball, John could always make me laugh. If he missed the ball, he would look at his paddle or grab another one from his bag. If he hit the ball over the net with a spin so his opponent was unable to return it, he was a happy camper. He loved to argue with me as to whether a ball was in or out. John was a trip, but we all loved to play with him.

Before and during games we often discussed a lot of things besides politics, like restaurants and ball games. One day before starting play I told John about a leak we had at the house. He said he could fix it with a clear caulk that he often used on construction jobs. John's paying job was as a carpenter. I said great. The next day, John showed up at our home in a pair of clean coveralls and the caulk. He carefully applied the material around two sets of French doors and said, "That'll be forty dollars." I didn't mind paying him but was a little surprised as I thought he was doing it as a friend.

To my surprise, when John's 70th birthday approached he invited my wife and I and several other pickleball players to a celebration at this country-style home in Upper Township on Tyler Road. We were asked to bring our own lawn chairs for sitting outside. And of course, we wouldn't come empty handed for the birthday boy. A bottle of wine would do fine.

Upon our arrival we unloaded our chairs and walked up the steps to his newly constructed deck where we were introduced to John's family and friends. On the deck was a large couch and several chairs with room for six. Within a few minutes several other pickleball players arrived with their wives. They included Ray Matricardi, who had worked with John on numerous construction projects, Ward Reese, one of the pickleball regulars, and Bruce Gorman, a retired local judge who graced us with his presence on the court when he felt like it.

As we gazed over the property in search of John, we spied him near his chicken coop picking up a large black snake with a piece of wood and tossing it into the brush. That scene sealed it for all our wives. Nobody was leaving the deck except to go home. There was plenty of food and drink for all on the deck and the ground level of the property. However, since our wives refused to leave their raised sanctuary, we were assigned the task of bringing them platters.

When COVID-19 forced the closing of the Upper Township Community Center, our weekly pickleball games with John came to an abrupt stop. We attempted to play outside at Caldwell Park, but that turned into a one and done experience due to the lack of players.

With the advent of the COVID vaccines, the Community Center reopened with certain restrictions for pickleball. You had to wear a mask when playing and you could only play there if you were from Upper Township or Ocean City. This greatly reduced the available player pool as many of the regular participants came from other towns like Millville, Rio Grande, Mays Landing, and Egg Harbor Township. Somehow, we managed to get four players on most days. These included John, Ward, Bob Swartz, and me. Slowly the restrictions were relaxed and you could play without a mask if you were vaccinated. John, being who he was, was the last one to get vaccinated.

Late in the summer of 2021 we learned that John had put his house up for sale and planned to move to either Northern Arizona or Tennessee. He felt it was too expensive to live in New Jersey and there were too many restrictions. In a way he believed if he moved west all he needed was a gun and a coonskin hat. With a shortage of homes across the country, John's home sold quickly and he received a great price for it. He also believed the housing market would soon bust and he could get a "good buy" on a house further west.

Having built kind of a "love/hate" relationship with John over several years, I couldn't let him leave without at least giving him a goodbye breakfast. I contacted several other pickleball players who enjoyed John's company and asked if they'd like to join me taking him to breakfast on his last day of play. Even Ward, who had missed the previous four weeks due to his wife's hip replacement, agreed to come. It was touch and go right up until the proposed morning for the breakfast at Dino's diner in Seaville, NJ. John wasn't sure he could even make it as settlement was being moved around. If he didn't make it, we would still have the breakfast and call it a "wake."

In the end, John moved things around and showed up to play his last few games of pickleball with us. Ward also showed as did several others including Maggie Ludgate, an English transplant,

171

and Matt Bechta who had only known John for a few months but enjoyed his company.

After playing several games we headed to Dino's just a few miles away. There we waited for John. We thought he was right behind us. As it turned out, Ward had misplaced his car keys and John ended up driving him to the diner. Ward had looked everywhere for his keys except the bottom pocket of his gym bag (That became a running joke for several weeks). Once there, we all related our stories about John, had a good laugh, and wished him well on his travels west.

Gone with the Wind

Twenty plus years ago, when we purchased our year-round home in Ocean City, we noticed a large amount of bird droppings on our cars, which we parked on the concrete pad at the back of our home. Many of the droppings came from the winged critters sitting on the wires along the back alley. In an attempt to thwart the assortment of winged creatures and their waste, after some research I decided to purchase a realistic-looking owl decoy with a rotating head and secure it on the highest point of the roof at the back of the house. Following the instructions on the decoy, I filled it with sand and sealed the base.

The only way to reach the high point on the roof, my chosen location for the owl, was by placing a ladder on the back deck of the house and carefully inching my way up the roof to the point. With a mixture of anxiety, fear, and excitement I was able to make my way up the roof and screw the base of the decoy into the shingles at the top. For two decades the mighty owl stood on the roof as a silent deterrent to the large black crows, sparrows, and pigeons. That all ended with the second nor'easter of 2022.

Three days after the storm, there were piles of snow everywhere. As we peered out our dining room window, we noticed a dark object in the snow near our outside shower. What was it? I took a snow shovel and made my way outside the door towards the shower. As I got closer, I could see what looked like wings. Could it be a Canadian goose who hit the house and froze to death? On closer examination it appeared to be our decoy owl, but the head was missing.

The easiest way to confirm my suspicions was to open the garage door and check the roof. Looking up where the decoy had stood for more than 20 years, I could see that it was gone, gone with the nor'easter winds and snow of 2022. A few days later I found the owl's head in another part of the yard along with a few other pieces. Thinking about the event, we were lucky the decoy fell to the side of our house rather than falling straight down and damaging our cars on the pad below. It was still protecting us even on its way down.

With the assistance of my son, Denny, we replaced the owl with another decoy when the weather broke. However, this time it is perched on the point over the garage and not the top roof. Something we reached without much fear and anxiety.

Chapter 7: Better Than the Alternative

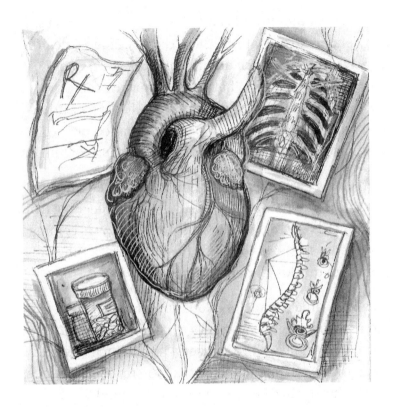

When I wake up in the morning with an ache in my hands or a pain in my back or someplace else, I wish for the days when I felt none of those things. I believe it was author George Bernard Shaw who said, "Youth is wasted on the young." This may be true. Often as a child and young man I felt invincible. However, today as I'm closer to eighty than seventy, a little pain here or there is better than the alternative.

Free Medical Assistance

As my baby boomer friends and I have aged, the main topic of many of our conversations these days tend to be health related. We often ask each other, "How are you feeling?" "What hurts today?" or "What doctor are you seeing this week?" Having worked as an instructional designer in the pharmaceutical field, I often impart information or suggestions, sometimes with an attempted sense of humor.

Here are a few examples. There was a time when my artist friend, Larry Stein, was in the hospital due to bleeding from the rectum. His doctors weren't sure where it was coming from. I offered to show up with a flashlight and a tube of super glue to quickly remedy the problem.

When a long-time friend, Joel Toussaint, was having problems swallowing food due to a narrowing of his throat, I volunteered to throw a rope over a tree branch to stretch his neck in one treatment rather than the three-step process offered by his doctor. For some reason he opted for the physician's approach.

Another friend, Neal, a CPA, was having a problem with his eyes. After 50+ years of doing tax returns, his eyelids were falling down, covering his eyes. He was going to have plastic surgery to correct the problem. I, again, offering to be of assistance, told him I could remedy the problem with super glue. There is nothing like it.

Aging is My Kryptonite

One thing I've learned about growing older is to try and avoid doing anything stupid, especially around the home. I have learned, sometimes the hard way, I'm no longer invincible. Like Superman I have a weakness. For him it was Kryptonite. For me it's aging. Things I used to do almost without thinking have become challenges and end up becoming bruises or disasters. It could be as simple as changing a light bulb standing on a chair. As a result of my loss of invincibility I think before I act. Here are a few examples. Use a ladder with someone there to hold it. Even standing on a ladder can be dangerous. My wife doesn't like me on ladders, especially without someone watching or bracing it.

How often have you attempted to reach something just out of your grasp on a shelf above your head? "Oh, just another inch or two," you say to yourself. Trying to reach that last spot on the wall that needs to be painted. Not holding on to a banister going up or down steps. The end result could be a fall and broken bones, or even worse. If you're on a blood thinner and hit your head the result could be a brain bleed.

There's a whole lot of things to think about in your seventies and beyond – if you're going to get there or stay around a little longer. For instance, shoveling snow without a back support, not watching your step coming on or off a curb, just shutting a cabinet door and scraping your arm or hand. In the past you wouldn't give it a second thought. However, now you do, because there's blood or a black and blue. It's something super glue can't fix. And don't forget about that cell phone and your surroundings. How many folks, young and old, have been tripped up while focused on the screen.

What about walking across a wet or freshly waxed floor, or not holding on to the handrail in the shower or tub? You're lucky if you can even get out of a bathtub safely (stick to a shower and hold on!). Even trying to stay active while not getting hurt takes some thought. I've learned not to try and go backwards when reaching for a pickleball over my head or just out of my reach. "Let it go," I say to myself. "It's just a game!" Losing a point is a lot less painful than a trip to the ER and spending several days in the hospital or months in a cast. Think about it before you do it!

One other thing for you my dog loving folks who love walking your pets. Within a week I heard three different stories about friends and relatives who were walking their dogs and either tripped or got caught up in the leash and fell. One severely sprained their ankle, another fell and broke an ankle, and the third ended up cracking two ribs when they fell. Think about getting a cat. Just kidding!

The Year of Dangerous Living

In the Mel Gibson film, *A Year of Living Dangerously*, journalist Guy Hamilton faces numerous threats as he seeks a story in Indonesia. I faced a few challenges and challenged myself to reach the age of 75. It was a real milestone for me. I was still active, playing pickleball, swimming, and playing beach volleyball, as long as my sons helped me up off the sand. During my yearly physical, my primary care physician, Dr. Horowitz, told me my heart was good. However, it was the year when the aches and pains of aging began rearing their creaking noises on a more frequent basis, literally from head to toe.

As I remember it, feeling like 75 started one morning on my right knee, immediately after my birthday. What a gift! For some reason the knee hurt just getting out of bed. It didn't feel much better after my daily morning exercise routine. Rubbing in Voltaren© Gel and taking an OTC pain reliever didn't help much either. When it didn't disappear within a few days, I called Dr, Krome, a doctor I knew at a local orthopedic practice in Somers Point for an appointment. You're lucky if you can get an appointment when you need one. It can be two weeks or much more.

As if the gods were watching over me, I got an appointment within 10 days. When I went, the doctor X-rayed both knees. It showed how the cartilage was narrowing in both and that someday I might need a replacement, but not now. I had arthritis. "What do you expect at 75?" I was told. It was acting up, and a cortisone shot should do the trick. Happily, it did.

As the knee began to feel better, I started my gardening routine. I went to Lowe's and purchased several bags of topsoil for my vegetable garden, as they were on sale (and I never like to miss a bargain). As I began loading the bags into the car, I began to feel a strain in my left eye. It felt like something was in there. The thought ran through my brain that I had a lifted things beyond my weight limit and torn the retina in my left eye. I had a tear several years earlier after getting hit in the eye with a volleyball. It was no fun.

Fearing the worst, I made an appointment with my eye doctor, whom I had just seen earlier in the week for my yearly checkup. With the gods still keeping watch over me, I timed my call right. I was told to come right over. The good doctor, Dr. Dunn, a specialist who teaches at Wills Eye in Philly, examined my eye, but could see nothing wrong. No retinal tear or anything. He suggested I use some OTC eye drops for a few days. If something changed, I should give him a call.

Two weeks after seeing the eye doctor, I went for my six-month dental check-up and cleaning. Based on the results of an x-ray, my dentist found a cavity under a crown, and it was deep. He initially believed I needed a root canal. How that problem was resolved is described in the next story. And while all this was taking place, COVID-19 reared its ugly head.

The Namath Benefit

I get a kick out of the TV commercials featuring Joe Namath and other over the hill athletes or once famous actors promoting medical advantage plans and telling me to call that 800 number to make sure I get all the benefits I'm entitled to. The benefits they often cite include such things as coverage for dental, vision, over the counter drugs, and transportation to and from a medical appointment. From experience I've learned you often have to fight to receive these benefits even if you are entitled to them. Sometimes it takes months and determination, a lot of determination.

Here's what I mean. At one of my twice-yearly regular dental check-ups, my In Network dentist, Dr. Poltorak, a really nice guy who goes the extra mile for you, noticed a cavity under a crown and set up an appointment to remedy the situation. After removing the crown, the dentist believed I needed a root canal, which he could not perform because it was very deep. His admin set up an appointment for me with a local endodontic specialist to perform the service. The cost would be $1425.00, for the service as this specialist was "out of network."

After removing the crown and taking an x-ray, the endodontist told me he was unable to perform the root canal. He felt it was too deep. He charged me $100 for the diagnosis and $25.00 for the x-ray. Not a big deal.

I then called my dentist and explained the situation. He told me I could either have the tooth extracted and get a bridge or do an implant. I opted for the extraction and a bridge. I also asked the dentist if he could recommend an In Network oral surgeon to perform the extraction. He had his admin research oral surgeons in the area. I also called my medical insurance company to get the name of an In-Network oral surgeon in the area. The insurance company gave me the name of 2 In-Network oral surgeons.

I called the dentist this time for his opinion of these 2 surgeons. The doctor was familiar with both but said one was in the process of moving her office. So, I elected to go with surgeon closest to my home.

After completing a patient questionnaire, I made an appointment for the extraction. I was told the fee would be $500 and I needed a referral from my regular dentist. A week later I went for the extraction. It was performed by another surgeon in the practice, not the one I thought would perform the procedure. Here's where the fun started. I had no idea, until weeks later that doctors are listed as In Network, not practices.

After the extraction was performed, I mailed a reimbursement form to my insurance company with all the requested information, including a copy of the paid invoices for the root canal consultation and extraction. Three weeks later I received an explanation of benefits from the insurance company's dental program saying neither of the two claims would be paid. I called the dental program that evening. It was explained to me that these two claims were not covered by them. However, I was entitled to $250.00 under my Medicare Advantage Reimbursement Program. The lady I spoke with also wondered why the documents were sent to her group. She suggested I contact the insurance company at the home office.

Feeling I was getting the runaround, I immediately called the insurance company. The representative I spoke with tried to pull up the claim form I submitted several weeks earlier but was unable to locate it. At her request, I emailed her copies of the reimbursement form I had submitted along with copies of the receipts. I received a note via email from her a short time later acknowledging that she had received the documents. The next day, I emailed the rep a note asking if she could tell me anything. She said I would get a call the next day. That call never came.

The next day, I called the insurance company again and spoke with another representative in the same department as the first one. I explained the entire situation once again. She asked me to resend the documents to a different email address, which I did.

After a week of not hearing anything, I called the insurance company again and explained the entire situation one more time. It was getting to the point where no one would speak to me. I let the situation sit for a few weeks as it was now Christmas time.

A few days after the new year, I called member services again after learning my claim was denied for the $250.00 reimbursement. I asked to speak to a supervisor to discuss my claim. I was told to email my information to another person, which I did once again.

Ten days later, I called member services to find out the status of my claim. I could get no information. I then called Dental Services and explained the situation to a representative. She set up a 3-way call with Member Services. We spoke with another rep. The lady from the dental program did the talking. We were told the claim was being processed. I was told to check back with Member Services in 30 days.

After 30 days I saw the claim was denied once again. I appealed the claim once again. This time I copied the information exactly from the company's website which stated the benefit of $250.00 I was entitled to "Reimbursement for certain dental procedures not covered by the dental program, including extractions."

A few weeks later I received a check from the insurance company for the $250.00 plus a few cents interest owned to me from the date I had originally filed the claim. I wonder if I had had Mr. Namath on my side things would have gone a lot faster. Maybe he could have told me the right play to call.

What's Up Doc?

As a kid going to Saturday matinees and watching Looney Tunes cartoons featuring Bugs Bunny was a lot of fun. In every cartoon, at a certain time Bugs, sometimes chewing on a carrot, would pop that famous question to Elmer Fudd, "What's up doc?" As I've moved into my 70s, that question has become relevant.

To check on my overall health, and make sure I'm alive, besides checking the obituaries on a daily basis, I do a yearly wellness physical. Because of insurance requirements, the visit is at least a year and a day after the previous year's visit. In the past, I would go for blood work a few weeks in advance and then sit down with Dr. Horowitz, my primary care physician, to discuss the results. Now, thanks to modern technology, I can review the blood work results online, ahead of the visit, and discuss any items of concern.

Though I was on great terms with my doctor, I was feeling kind of hyper about the visit on this particular day in August. When it was time for my appointment, I went to an exam room with his medical assistant, Charlene. She checked my weight and then I sat down and waited for Dr. Horowitz to come in.

Within a few minutes, the doctor arrived, and we began to discuss the results. The key results we generally reviewed was my PSA due to BPH, or an enlarged prostate, something I inherited from my father, Louie. One thing that seemed odd was an indication I was below average on vitamin D, which could easily be remedied with a single D3 pill every day.

Next, Dr. H checked my blood pressure and for some reason it was high. To confirm it, he had his nurse practitioner, Jill, give me an EKG. Yep, my heart rate was elevated.

We then sat down and discussed my options. He could start me on some pill to monitor the condition. However, I would have to stop all activities until there was a solution. That meant no pickleball, pool or beach volleyball for some time. My other option was to go to the emergency room at Shore Memorial Hospital, immediately, and have an overnight observation stay. I opted for the ER and the overnight stay, not wanting to have to stop all my activities. Dr. H said he would call ahead to the hospital to let them know I was coming.

I immediately went home, told my wife what had transpired, and packed an overnight bag with toiletries and clean underwear. We then drove to Shore Memorial, parked the car, and went in through the Emergency Room entrance. Inside I filled out a questionnaire and provided my insurance information. Then we waited several hours before being called. While there I sat near a girl with a COVID-19 molecule tattoo on her leg. That didn't make me feel really safe, but we had masks on. Luckily, I wasn't having a heart attack or chest pains.

For about the next three hours we sat in the waiting room. People were coming in on a continuous basis. There were kids with fevers and throwing up, pseudo athletes with sprained arms and legs, and a lady carried in on a stretcher who they brought back into the ER immediately.

When they finally called my name, we traveled into the dark crevasses of the ER. There were so many twists and turns you would need several pounds of Reese's Pieces to find your way back out. Eventually we were led to a small room at the back of the ER. It wasn't much larger than a closet. It did have a hospital bed and several devices. I was asked to remove my outer clothing and get into the bed, which I did.

A short time later, I was hooked up to a monitor. It showed my heart rate at 137 bpm. My wife took out her cellphone and took a picture of the reading and sent it to my daughter-in-law, Michelle, a critical care nurse. In the meantime, I was just lying there, really feeling nothing but a little hyper and a little hungry. While I was waiting for someone to do something, different medical staff kept walking in and looking at the monitor. It was like I was an oddity.

Before long, a nurse, Jennifer, finally came in, checked my vitals and hooked me up to an IV. I told her to please do it right the first time. I explained that too many times I've had blood taken and the vampire says, "Oops." Luckily, Jennifer did it right the first time. She found a vein. Then, she checked the monitor. I was still at 137.

Seeing where my bpm was, she gave me some meds through an IV, which quickly brought it down to 62. After that I just laid there for what seemed like hours. At one point, a doctor walked in and noticed my legs. She said, "Your legs are swollen." I replied, "No. I'm an athlete and have always had muscular legs." Jennifer was in the room at the time and heard the conversation. She asked me if she could use that line if someone commented about her legs.

As it became later in the evening, I told my wife to go home, as I was fine. An hour later an aide came in and told me I would be staying overnight. They just needed to find me a room. Not being able to help myself, I asked, "Can I get one with a view?"

Long story, short, I finally got into a room on the second floor around 10 pm. I couldn't tell if it had a view or not as it was dark. Since it was way past mealtime, I was offered some juice and crackers, which I accepted as my stomach was making some complaints.

I was still connected to the IV, and the nurse hooked me up to a heart monitor to check my vitals. There were several other medical devices in the room for what exact purpose I didn't know. Between them and the noise from the corridor outside my door, I was up most of the night.

About midnight, an aide came by for blood work. Luckily, I had an IV they could use, so there would be no other "oops" moments.

When morning came, a member from the food service staff gave me menus for breakfast and lunch. They were both salt free. Breakfast wasn't bad, pancakes and toast, but lunch was on the bland side as I didn't have many choices being a finicky eater.

After breakfast, I was supposed to get an echocardiogram. However, it was delayed for a while as the lab was backed up due to problems from the day before. Eventually, I was taken for the test. There were two technicians, Bob, and Harry. They were nice guys and knew what they were doing. They even laughed at some of my jokes. I love to tell jokes and stories as they help to keep me calm. After the echo, I was taken back to my room to await the results. I also had some additional blood work.

After eating some of my bland lunch, a dry turkey sandwich, I was visited by a hospitalist, and then a cardiologist from Penn Medicine. The cardiologist explained that I apparently had arterial flutter when I came in the day before, but my heart rate was now back to normal and there was no damage to the organ. He didn't know why it happened or if it would reoccur. He suggested putting me on a once-a-day beta blocker and low-dose blood thinner twice a day, and to see him again in 30 days. I agreed to his terms and was discharged shortly after that.

The event shook my family and my nurse daughter-in-law ordered me a knock-off Fitbit which would allow me to check my heart rate at any time. I started wearing it when it arrived and now use it as a watch and to check my bpm when I'm playing pickleball. Apparently, my resting bpm is around 56 which has concerned my wife. She wonders whether I'm really alive or not, as hers is regularly in the 70s. However, my PCP says that's okay and tells me I'm still kicking.

The Spine Tingler

Oh, the joys of getting older. As I mentioned earlier, it's better than the alternative. I've had an aching back for many years and I know where it came from – a hit in the back when I played rugby on the day my first son was born. Occasionally it can act up. This time I believe it was caused by sitting on backless bleachers on a football field for three hours at a high school graduation, plus a couple of hours of driving.

That night, after our return to Ocean City, my right ankle began hurting when I got into bed. The pain kept me up most of the night. I had been treated in the past for foot problems by a foot and ankle specialist. The earliest appointment I could get was a week later. The doctor gave me a cortisone shot and prescribed a regimen of prednisone. The pain eased for about a week, then returned. I called the doctor's office and was told to give the treatment more time.

Long story short, time did not improve the pain. Every night when I went to sleep, within a few minutes the ankle was generating pain. As a result, I was unable to get much sleep and was awake most of the night.

Not getting any relief, I decided to try acupuncture which was not covered by my health insurance. I went for three treatments on my right ankle over a period of 6 weeks. After the third treatment, with no easing of the night pain, the acupuncturist concluded he couldn't help me. I was thinking of trying an Indian medicine man next.

Since that wasn't practical (I didn't know any shamans from the local tribe) I met with my favorite PCP, Dr. Horowitz. I explained my pain, and he examined my ankle closely, moving it in different directions. There was no pain or ache as he twisted the ankle. He determined that the pain was "referred" even though I didn't ask for one. It was coming from another area (my back) and being directed to my ankle at night when I was lying down.

A few days later I went back to the foot specialist. He examined my ankle and also determined the problem was from referred pain and not the ankle itself. To prove his diagnosis, he ordered an X-ray of the right ankle which was completed a few days later. The foot specialist also gave me another cortisone shot and prescribed another regimen of prednisone. The pain only subsided for a few days. The X-rays showed no arthritis in the right ankle.

Since it was believed the problem was in my lower back, I went to a local chiropractic physician, Dr. O'Rourke, for five treatments over several weeks to relieve the pain as I was still not sleeping at night due to the ankle pain.

During this experience I tried almost every over-the counter-treatment I could find, or was advertised on TV, including Advil©, Aleve©, Tylenol©, Voltaren©, Biofreeze©, EMU Oil®, Tiger Balm©, Epsom Salt Rub, and ZIMs™ Max Freeze to relieve the pain. If you can name it, I tried it with little lasting success.

Since I was receiving no relief from the night pain, my PCP requested an MRI of my Lumbar Spine. We thought it was a great idea. However, the request was turned down by my big bad insurance company. I had many friends with the same experience. Undaunted, I met with my doctor again. He carefully examined me and once again recommended the MRI to locate the exact spot for a steroid injection to alleviate the pain.

It was turned down once again. This time the bad guys recommended that I do 6 weeks of physical therapy first. I couldn't see the purpose as I stretch out every morning for fifteen minutes and work out (exercising and treading water) for 45 minutes in the swimming pool three days a week. I have been doing that for almost twenty years.

Knowing I really needed an MRI to locate the exact spot needed for an injection or therapy, my doctor, also undaunted, held a peer-to-peer conference regarding the MRI with one of insurance company physicians. He presented our case for the test and was led to believe it was finally being approved.

I called the doctor's office a few days later and was told to go ahead and make an appointment for the MRI with the medical imaging company that provides the test in our area. The office was only waiting for a final approval. I made an appointment for the following Monday at 4:30 pm.

I followed up with doctor's office the next day. They were still waiting for the final approval. On Wednesday of that week, I received a call from the imaging company saying they still had not received approval. Not wanting to leave anything to chance, I called the insurance company to find out what I could. After waiting on the phone for over 30 minutes I was told that Dr. Horowitz's office needed to send over additional documents. I asked, "What documents?" They couldn't tell me. By this time the doctor's office was closed. You know Wednesday afternoons many like to golf.

On Thursday morning, I reached out to Dr. Horowitz's office. They told me that they had spoken with someone familiar with the case and should be receiving the authorization on Friday. That morning I called the doc's office once again to find out if they had received the approval. Apparently, now they were told they had to send additional information. They did. Thank heavens they like me over there.

At this point in time, a little frustrated, I decided to go ahead with the MRI and pay for it myself. I had been in pain for over three months unable to sleep in bed or tell many jokes. I spent most of every night and the early morning hours in a chair. Money-wise, I had already spent the amount the MRI would cost me out-of-pocket on acupuncture and chiro treatments to remedy the problem. I couldn't wait any longer as insurance people with no real medical knowledge played games with my life.

Long story, short. The insurance approval came about two hours before I was scheduled to get the MRI that Monday afternoon. But the best is yet to come. I arrived at the imaging facility about 30 minutes in advance of my time to fill out any paperwork needed. As I sat in the waiting area, I noticed the lights flickering on and off in the building. I thought to myself, "This isn't a good sign."

At about 4:30, my scheduled time for the test, a technician called my name. I stood up and said, "Here I am." She said, "Mr. Zakroff, please sit down. We're having a problem with the electricity and may have to send you to another facility. I'll let you know in a few minutes where things stand." I shook my head and broke out laughing. I almost get to "the promised land" and this happens. I'm sure the good lord was having fun with this. I just didn't know he was an electrician.

As it turned out, they managed to get the power straightened out within the next 30 minutes. I then went in and had the test. It was something I had never experienced before with noises and cranks and buzzing. I imagined this was what it felt like to be buried alive in a coffin.

The next day I received a call from Dr. Horowitz. He wanted to discuss the results. He opened the discussion by saying, "We didn't see what we wanted to see." Startled, I replied, "What!" He then added, "Just kidding." He was getting back at me for all my jokes and stories. Based on his observations, I had some damage to several vertebrae, but could get relief with a steroid shot. He then recommended two orthopedic specialists at the Rothman Institute who I could call to administer the shot. What happened next is another tale.

Can I Play the Piano?

Following the successful MRI, I played telephone roulette with the Rothman phone line. Eventually I reached a live person, Kathy. I gave her my name, birthdate, phone number, and insurance information. She then asked me to wait to make sure they took my insurance.

After a few minutes on hold, Kathy came back on the phone and said, "We don't accept your insurance." I explained that my wife had a double knee replacement two years earlier at Rothman using the same insurance. Kathy told me contracts change each year and maybe things had changed. I then asked, "What can I do?" She told me to contact my insurance company and see who they would recommend. A little peeved, I hung up and followed her instructions.

A few minutes later, while on the phone with my insurance company, I heard another call coming in. I put the insurance company on hold and answered it. It was Kathy from Rothman calling back. She had made a mistake. They did take my insurance. I then gave her the names of the two orthopods my doctor had recommended and asked which one I could get the earliest appointment.

As it turned out that was 6 weeks with Dr. Axelrod. I took it. I then called my PCP's office and informed them of my progress. Charlene on Dr. Horowitz's staff suggested that I call Rothman every day to find out if there were any cancellations. I took her advice and called every day for several weeks in advance of my appointment. Each day I received the same response. No cancellations.

Then, two days before my scheduled appointment, I received a call from Dr. Axelrod's office. They had an opening the next day. I said, "I'll take it!" I had high hopes of getting an injection on my first visit, but that wasn't in the cards.

On the day of my initial appointment, I drove to The Rothman Building in English Creek. After a short wait, I met with Dr. Alyson Axelrod, a D.O. with Rothman. I brought with me a narrative of the pain and trepidations I had over the previous three months. She reviewed the results of my MRI, examined by back and my ability to move my legs and ankles. She then made a sketch of where my problem was which made it easy to understand. I explained to her that Dr. Horowitz thought a steroid shot in my lower back would help relieve the pain in my ankle and allow me to sleep at night.

We talked about options. I didn't think physical therapy was the route to go. I wanted the shot. She agreed, but I learned I couldn't get one that day. Steps and procedures needed to be followed. Ah, modern medicine and regulations.

After our meeting, Dr. Axelrod's assistant took me to the Surgical Coordinator. There I learned I needed to get clearance for the shot from my cardiologist, Dr. Persad. I also had to stop my blood thinner for three days in advance of the injection. I would also need someone to drive me to and from the office on the day of the procedure. The earliest I could get the shot was in three weeks. I hoped I could last that long.

When the day arrived, my wife drove me to Rothman and waited. It didn't take long for me to see Dr. Axelrod. After her assistant checked my vitals, she guided me to the procedure room where Dr. Axelrod was waiting. She explained I was going to get three needles. One was a dye to help with tracing the locations of the shot, plus two addition injections of the steroid.

I hardly felt the first two shots. However, the third went down my right leg to my ankle. She hit the correct nerve. I tried not to show pain or yell even though it was intense. After a few seconds the pain dissipated. Then I asked that famous question, humorous people ask after an operation, "Can I now play the piano?"

Dr. Axelrod admitted she didn't know how long the shot would last. There were no guarantees. She said, "For some people it's a homerun. For others, not so much." I was hoping for at least a single or maybe a double. The injection did help, and its effects have lasted for several months.

Anyone Who Wants One Can Get One

In December of 2020, then President Trump announced that anyone who wanted a COVID-19 vaccine could get one when they became available. If you were senior citizens like my wife and I and millions of other Americans, it wasn't that easy early on. It was a real challenge. We tried every available avenue. We signed up on the government and New

Jersey websites to get appointments and waited. We tried to get on the site of the local supermarket where we shopped for appointments, but it was always full. We checked with our personal physician's office. However, they had no available information.

Then, one day at the Ocean City Aquatic & Fitness Center, where we were allowed to swim on a limited basis during the pandemic, a friend, Dave Jungblut, a college astronomy instructor, gave me a cellphone number he had received from another friend, who said they had managed to get a COVID shot a few days ago. When I got home, I tried the number. The phone rang and rang and rang. No one answered. However, I saved the number just in case.

Over the next few days, I checked all the sites I had tried before: state, federal, and supermarket. All with no success. Figuring I had nothing to lose, I tried the phone number Dave had given me earlier. To my surprise, a lady answered. A little taken back, I asked the important question, "Do you give the COVID-19 vaccinations?" "Yes, we do." She answered. "This is your lucky day."

I had no idea to whom or to where I was calling. All I knew they were in our area code and within traveling distance. I've had friends who traveled hundreds of miles to get their shots during the pandemic.

As luck would have it, we were able to make appointments for the next afternoon and the facility was a regional clinic only 25 minutes away in a strip mall. After filling out a few forms and providing our insurance information, we were directed to small waiting area with several other people who had also lucked out. Within 20 minutes we had rolled up our sleeves and each received our first dose of the Moderna vaccine along with a date and time for our second shots.

As a result of our good fortune, I supplied the phone number to several other friends who were able to their shots at the same location. Trump may have been right saying that anyone who wanted to get a COVID-19 vaccination could get one, but you needed to carefully read the fine print under his words, and work like hell to make it actually happen.

Chapter 8: Random Thoughts

Some stories are unique and don't fit in any one place. A number are true, others like creative ideas and poems just popped into my head. However, I feel they are worth telling and require their own special place. Here are several for your reading pleasure.

An Apple from the Big Apple

Today, when you want to buy a new computer, you can go online to order one from Dell, HP, or Amazon, or visit a Staples, Office Max, or Apple store. However, early on, that wasn't the case.

My first computer was an Apple 2 plus which I purchased in the 1970's. I had learned about computers from my friend Dan DeSantis. Dan was always into gadgets and electronics, as well as model trains and antique cars. At the time there were no Apple stores. Instead, folks were selling Apples out of their apartments if you wanted one. Dan had purchased his that way. With an address in hand I made plans to travel to New York City on a weekend.

One Saturday morning I boarded a Trailways bus at exit four of the NJ Turnpike. It took me to the Port Authority building in New York City. From there, I walked several blocks to an apartment building. The address I had received from Dan.

I entered the building and took the elevator up to the fourth floor. Once there I hunted for the apartment number Dan had given me and knocked on the door. A bearded young man of about 35 opened the door and asked, "Can I help you?" I told him I was there to purchase an Apple and the additional equipment I needed, which according to Dan included a monitor, hard drive, dot matrix printer, and some floppy disks.

He let me in the apartment which I could see was full of computer boxes and peripherals. I told him my needs and he gave me a price for the items. Wanting the equipment, I said,

"Okay." I expected to take the computer and related equipment with me. However, he said, "These are only demos. I can ship you your components in the next week or so."

I was a little skeptical but agreed. I wrote him a check for the full amount, got a receipt, and left. All the way back to the bus station and home I wondered if I had been snookered. In the end, I wasn't. Several boxes arrived two weeks later with everything I had ordered. Dan came over to my house and helped me set everything up. He also gave me a quick tutorial. I was now in the computer age, as long as I did what the computer allowed me to do. Not the other way around.

Swimming at the Biltmore

When I began my new career as an instructional designer in the pharmaceutical industry, during the late 1990's, I knocked on a lot of doors in New York City in search of work. One company I hit it off with was RJO productions. RJO hired me to design eight workshops for a new cancer drug being promoted by a large pharma company.

My assignment included going onsite for the product introduction meeting at the famous Biltmore Hotel outside of Phoenix, AZ. There are several things I remember well about the experience. They included a great deal of friction among the client team before and onsite as well as being charged almost $20.00 for a room-service provided hamburger. I always check out the burgers.

However, my most memorable moment came when racing through the hotel lobby for a client meeting and catching my foot on the edge of the in-lobby aquarium. As a result of my haste, I ended up half in the water. After creating quite a splash, I laid there for a few seconds considering what had just happened, trying to feel my arms and legs to make sure everything was still working. I also considered the embarrassment of where I was and what had just happened.

Half soaked and physically bruised along my right shoulder, elbow and arm, I slowly picked myself up. I then slowly drudged my way back to my hotel room to check myself out and change my clothes. Shying away from onlookers, I made my way to the elevator and to my room on the fourth floor. Once in the room, I went into the bathroom and slowly removed my shirt from my now aching arm and shoulder. Gazing in the mirror, I was black and blue from the top of my shoulder and down my arm to my wrist. I could move everything and at least I wasn't bleeding on the outside.

For the rest of the meeting, I kept a low profile and avoided the center of the lobby, just in case any of the fish in the aquarium were looking for a meaty meal. I always wondered whether I had actually tripped by my own doing or had been tossed by one of the many ghosts said to haunt that famous hotel.

Boardwalk Empire

Remember the HBO series crime drama, "Boardwalk Empire," which ran from 2010 to 2014? The story focused on Atlantic City at the dawn of Prohibition. It was a place where the rules didn't apply. And the man who ran things -- legally and otherwise – was the town's treasurer, Enoch "Nucky" Thompson. He was equal parts politician and gangster. Nucky worked closely with his brother Elias, Atlantic City's sheriff, and a crew of ward bosses and local tough guys. During the series Nucky gained a reputation as the man to see for illegal alcohol. He did business with all the top gangsters of the time -- Al Capone, Lucky Luciano, "Big Jim" Colosimo -- and he did it well.

I enjoyed watching the series. However, what caught my attention was the mention of the different hotels on the Atlantic City Boardwalk at the time. It seems the gangsters were always meeting at one hotel or another on several occasions to discuss business. The reason this mention perked my ears was that I knew my Aunt Tedda's family, the Goldbergs, owned and operated hotels on the Boardwalk. I wondered if they knew Nucky. With a little research I learned it was after Nucky's time.

The Book of Nasty Letters

"The pen is mightier than the sword" is a metonymic adage, created by English author Edward Bulwer-Lytton in 1839, indicating that the written word is more effective than violence as a tool for communicating a point. In fact, I also said that in my first book. I also found that it can be true – sometimes. What I didn't tell you was that I started writing a book full of "nasty" letters that folks could use as models to get some form of satisfaction from a company. The book was going to be based on successes I had in getting positive resolutions to problems I had with different products and services. I became pretty good at writing "nasty" letters, even writing some for family and friends.

Based on my successes, I created a working list of almost 50 "nasty" letters I could model for consumers to gain satisfaction when facing a large company without having to resort to a lawyer or going to court. My list included airlines, appliances, builders, carpet manufacturers, equipment, food products, hotels, insurance companies, and restaurants.

My real letters weren't totally "nasty." They relied on facts, a nudge about public opinion and possible negative publicity, and some humor. Overall, I was about 80% successful in my writings. However, this was another product I put on the back shelf as I became very busy with my occupation as an instructional designer. The real jobs paid better than just taking a chance on an idea that the sharks on Shark Tank would endorse and support. As time permits, this could be my next project.

The Hat – Delayed and Defective

A few years ago, out of the blue, I received a catalog from the Lands' End clothing company. Not normally a catalog buyer, what caught my eye was a heavy weight red ski jacket with navy blue cuffs and a white fleece lining. It was on sale for half price. I wanted to be sure the jacket fit, as I figured I needed an XL based on the sizing chart in the catalog.

I then checked the location of their brick and mortar stores. The closest one was in Cherry Hill, NJ, about a 70-minute drive from Ocean City. I also called the company's 800 number to see what the shipping charges would be, versus the drive. Shipping was eight dollars. I weighed the price of the ride through heavy traffic and tolls vs. placing an order. Eight dollars was a lot better than the ride.

Long story short, the jacket arrived in a few days and fit well. However, now I needed a matching hat for the jacket to keep my balding head warm during the winter months. The red one in the catalog was heavy and had ear flaps, something I had not used since childhood, and priced rather high, in my mind.

As a result, I started to look around for the head cover on Amazon and several local stores, even some on the boardwalk. Many of the red hats on Amazon were Trump 45 or MAGA hats. I would never place an item like that on my head. My honorable number two son, Dennis, was attuned to my needs and ordered a red hat for me, based on a picture he saw on the Amazon website. The hat was supposed to arrive in a few days. It took more than 10.

When it finally did arrive, I quickly opened the package and to my surprise, the back of the hat had "Trump 45" on it. This was not visible in the picture. As a result, I quickly returned it. When asked for a reason, I replied "delayed and defective."

Favorite Flicks

Having been raised on Saturday afternoon matinees, I developed a love of films. There are certain films I can watch repeatedly and never get bored even though I know exactly what's going to happen. I also hate remakes. Seldom do they measure up to the originals.

Take for instance the 1960 western The Magnificent Seven, a classic, based on a Japanese film called the Seven Samurai. The 60's version starred Yule Brenner, Steve McQueen, Charles Bronson, James Colburn, and Robert Vaughn, with Eli Wallach as Calvera, the bad guy and leader of the Mexican outlaws. This classic is tough to beat, and the soundtrack is fantastic. The later version with Denzel Washington just doesn't cut it for me. Putting together such a group of talented actors like those in the original would almost be impossible today. Just consider their salaries.

Another great western I enjoy watching is Red River featuring John Wayne, Montgomery Clift, Walter Brennan, and Joanne Dru. It was released in 1948. Wayne is at his best as a rancher driving a herd of cattle north after the civil war. Again the remake, with James Arness, in my opinion, doesn't make the grade. One other Wayne western I can watch repeatedly is The Searchers.

Along the line of remakes, what about the original "7 Days in May" with Kirk Douglas and Burt Lancaster? Another case where the remake doesn't cut the mustard. The same is true for "War of the Worlds," even though it featured Tom Cruise. I had to see the original three times as a child before I sat through the whole thing. It scared the pants off of me. Another great sci-fi film was the original "The Day the Earth Stood Still." The acting was phenomenal. All the remake had was more special effects.

As you can tell, westerns aren't the only flicks I like or can watch several times. There's "Casablanca" with Humphrey Bogart and "Mr. Holland's Opus" with Richard Dryfus, which always brings a tear to my eye. Have you ever watched Stanley and Livingstone with Spencer Tracy, a classic black and white film? What about "Patton," with George C. Scott, one of the greatest war movies ever made. Nobody would attempt a remake. Who else could play the part?

God has a Sense of Humor

I always believed that God has a sense of humor. He enjoys playing games with my mind. I can't remember how many times I walked into the locker room after swimming at the Aquatic Center in Ocean City to change my clothes or to get out of a wet bathing suit. There would be only one other person in the room and his locker was on top of mine.

How about when you go shopping at the supermarket? You get in a line to pay for your groceries and every other one is at least 3 or 4 persons deep, full of loaded shopping carts. You wait patiently in line, and then another cashier opens up and someone beats you to it.

How often do you fix something around the house – getting it perfect – and then something else breaks or requires your attention. What about when a light bulb goes out and you don't have a spare with the same wattage?

I love it when I'm cutting my small patch of grass with my battery-powered edger/weedwhacker, I only have a few feet to go, and the charge is exhausted.

The best one of all is when the smoke detector goes off at 3:00 am in the morning on a 12-foot ceiling in the bedroom. The only way to reach it is with the nine-foot ladder in the garage. Of course, you can't ignore it. It just keeps beeping, and you can hear the sound through the bedroom door.

The only solution is to get up, go to the garage, and bring in the nine-foot ladder. Then grab a new 9-volt battery and replace the bugger. After completing the task you try to go back to sleep. Good luck at accomplishing that feat!

Lasting Friendships

As a freelancer and small business owner most of my life, I've been limited in the number of people I call good friends. I still talk several times a year with several folks I met growing up, like Bob Stein, who lived a few doors away. Bob became a cardiologist and lives on the West Coast. Besides getting old, Bob never changes much. Plus, he still has his hair, which is more than I can say about myself.

There is also Mel Strieb. Mel comes from a well-educated family. His father was a doctor with the Philadelphia Health Department and his brothers, Bert and Jay taught at several local colleges. Mel himself has many talents and worked in aerospace and education. He is a man with many interests including the Peace Corps, archeology, and music. He also has a very distinct voice. Several years ago, I was having lunch with a client in Whitemarsh, PA when I heard this voice from across the dining room. It was Mel. I'd recognize his voice anywhere.

One other fellow from the old neighborhood I correspond with is Herb Levin. He now lives in Florida. Herb helped me do a final edit on my first book, and we exchange jokes via email.

Once in a while I come across some names from the past and pictures on Facebook like Jeff Lucas who lived on the next street, Andrews Avenue. Jeff lives in South Jersey and went into real estate. There's also Jerry Litvin, a friend from elementary school. Jerry became a pharmacist and had three wives. He once told me based on those experiences he became an expert on diamond rings. Last I heard, Jerry had retired and was living in Florida.

There are also a few friends from high school I stay in contact with, like Neal Cupersmith, the senior partner in a New Jersey accounting firm. Neal keeps talking about retiring but isn't sure what he'd do with himself if he actually did it. One other friend from high school is Larry B. Stein, a medical illustrator, dog breeder and show judge, who has traveled around the world judging different breeds. Larry recently moved to the middle of Virginia where cell service isn't too great, so we communicate via smoke signals.

A few other folks I call friends and stay in contact with include Joel Toussaint, who I met playing volleyball during the late 1970's. Joel worked for a South Jersey auto dealership in their training department for many years. When they let him go, he managed to stay busy working numerous jobs including delivering auto parts, working at a call center, and being a teacher's aide. We try to meet for lunch every few weeks but never talk politics.

Two other folks I call friends are from my business days. They include Nate Rosenblatt, a fast-thinking writer still working from home into his late 70's. Nate and I collaborated on a number of projects over the years and he still enjoys the challenge.

Marcy Altimano, on the other hand, was originally a training producer. I still remember the day she called me back in the 1990's and needed a fast turnaround on a project. We worked together for five years before I ever met her in person. Marcy moved to Arizona several years ago from Maplewood, NJ, and has switched from production to instructional design. She too talks about retiring but hates to turn down a project.

Never Call Anyone Stupid

One of my favorite expressions is "May the Good Lord keep one hand over my mouth and the other on my shoulder." It's something I learned the hard way.

It all started after a successful yearly meeting for a pharmaceutical company using the Amazing Race conceit I designed for them. Based on the positive feedback from the session, the communications company I was working with was hired to do the following year's meeting without having to bid on it. As a result of my idea, I was asked to work on the next one. I was flying high. Too high!

When it came time to begin work on the new meeting, I was on the phone with an administrative assistant from the company. As we talked, and I asked her questions, the responses I was getting made no sense. Becoming frustrated with the call, I asked, "Are you stupid?" It just spilled out. I couldn't believe I said it.

Within fifteen minutes of finishing that call, I received another. This was from my project manager, Joanne. She wanted to know what I had said to the admin. I explained the situation and was told I should never talk to the client directly again. I had cooked my own goose.

After that incident, I printed out my favorite saying in large type and pinned it on the bulletin board above my phone. Lesson learned – The hard way.

The Prime Directive

If you're a fan of Star Trek, you're probably familiar with "The Prime Directive:" Do not interfere with the civilization you are observing in any way so as to not affect their evolution as a species. I don't know how many episodes from the original TV series, Next Generation, as well as later versions and feature films stressed the importance of following this rule and the possible dangers of violating it.

However, today, with all the discussions, investigations, and photographic evidence of more advanced civilizations watching us, I wish they would violate such a directive (If they had one) and come to the rescue of people like the Ukrainians and the Kurds. I'm sure Putin and his cronies would wet their pants if a fleet of flying saucers suddenly appeared above Ukraine and totally neutralized their forces.

Consider the theory from UFO believers that we are being observed by more advanced species from far away star systems. Also, understand that sometimes I get a feeling of "deja'vu," like I've been here before. Could humankind have advanced this far in the past and wiped itself out? Has this been done several times before? Think about it. The Earth is several billion years old, and humans just keep doing the same stupid things repeatedly. Is history destined to repeat itself once again?

Are our alien observers watching and hoping to see if we can eventually get over the hump and learn to get along with each other? Or are they going to have to start the experiment all over again? Hoping for a different result from doing the same experiment over and over again without making a change is insane. Maybe they'll change the creatures they're working with in hopes of a better result. Think "Planet of the Apes."

Well-Read Tomatoes

Having a somewhat green thumb inherited from my mother, I plant a small vegetable garden every year. I built a raised garden about 3-feet by 5-feet and surrounded it on three sides by chicken wire to keep the birds and rabbits at bay in our Ocean City yard. I have a couple of removable wooden boards in the front of the bed which provides a protected entrance to the plot.

The crops in my little backyard garden don't vary much from year to year. It could be basil or lettuce, and some type of those famous Jersey red tomatoes. I don't eat them, but the rest of the family does. Though there are many varieties of tomatoes available, over the past few years I've settled on Better Boy Tomatoes versus Big Boys or Rutgers. The Better Boys have produced the largest crop of fruit I have ever had in both size and number.

Late in the season with climate change and unusually warm weather the vines often become overgrown but are still producing. By the end of October, I often remove the plants as insects get more fruit to eat than us. However, I harvest many of the green tomatoes and carefully wrap them in newspaper. Then I place them in brown paper bags to ripen. When asked by friends why I use that approach, I reply, "I wrap them in newspaper, so they have something to read while they are ripening."

A Zakroff Fable -How the Tortoise Beat the Hare

Just as writers adapt the works of other scribes before them to modern times and situations, I attempted the practice several years ago based on one of Aesop's Fables. Watching several TV commercials for muffler and brake franchises and thinking about the time required for the repair, I came up with an idea for waiting room programs for kids. Here is one based on "The Tortoise and the Hare" and how the tortoise really won.

Once upon a time, actually some time ago, there lived a hare named Harry who could run like the wind. Harry was really quick. He could run from here to there in a snap. Harry liked to brag about how fast he was and teased other animals into racing him.

He beat the lion, the tiger, and the bear. And after he beat them, he'd laugh at them. Having raced and beaten just about every animal in the forest, he was becoming bored. So, he decided to check over his racing list to see who hadn't given him a run.

It seemed like the only creature in the forest he hadn't raced was Tim Tortoise, old slow but sure. "That's it!" He thought. "I'll challenge the tortoise. It's not much of a contest, but it would be a race."

Making his way through the forest, Harry saw the tortoise and said, "Hey, Tim, how about a race?" Tim looked at the dragster, "Man! What are you after? We all know you're the fastest. How much glory is there in beating a tortoise?"

Seeing that it wasn't going to be easy to get Tim to race, Harry began to tease him about the way he looked, the way he talked, and the way he walked.

Tim started to lose his temper and before he knew what he was doing, he said, "I'll race you, you rabbit."

At the agreed upon time the whole forest turned out to see the race between the tortoise and the hare. Even the lion, the tiger and the bear were there.

The wise old owl, Hoot, was going to be the judge. As both contestants reached the starting point, Hoot fired his pistol. The hare was off in a cloud of dust.

The hare, knowing it was going to be an easy race, decided to stop at his favorite restaurant for a bowl of carrot soup, and a slice of carrot cake.

Meanwhile, Tim was slowly making his way down the road. Now just by chance, it seems, the route of the race happened to pass by a Mydis muffler shop. And the manager happened to be looking outside as Tim went by. Seeing how slow Tim was traveling the manager went outside to talk with him.

"Gee, Tim, for a fellow your size, you travel pretty slow," said the manager. "Well, if you had to carry a heavy shell like this over potholes and rough roads, you'd move pretty slow yourself."

"Have you had your shocks checked lately?" Asked the manager. "What are shocks? asked the tortoise. "They help give you a smoother ride, hold the road, and carry your load better," said the manager.

"I don't think mother nature ever gave me any of them," remarked Tim. "Well, maybe we can help you out," said the Mydis man.

Tim went into the shop with the manager. The manager checked his model catalog on the computer and went into the stock room. A few minutes later he came out with a box labeled "Super Tortoise Shock Absorbers." "These should work for you," he said.

Having been trained in shock absorber installation, the shop mechanics had Tim fixed up in a jiffy. Tim thanked the manager for his help and quick service. He then roared off down the road towards the finish line.

Meanwhile, Harry was just finishing his soup and getting ready to order dessert when he saw a cloud of dust pass the restaurant. He looked again and couldn't believe his eyes. That wasn't a cloud of dust going smoothly down the road. It was Tim the Tortoise. Out Harry went after the load-balanced tortoise.

But it was too late. Thanks to Mydis and their quick and friendly service, the tortoise had done the impossible. He had beaten the hare.

And that is the true story of how Mydis helped the tortoise to beat the hare and establish the need for fast service carrot soup restaurants.

The Muffler Tree

Growing up I often heard the expression, "Money doesn't grow on trees." That got me thinking about other things that don't really grow on trees but would be fund to imagine if they did. One of those thoughts turned into the following little piece that went along with the previous story.

"Billy, finish setting the table for dinner. Your father will be home from work soon." said his mother.

A few minutes later Billy heard a loud booming noise coming from the driveway. "Dad's home." he said.

At the dinner table, Billy's mother said to her husband, "I think you need a new muffler for that car, dear."

Billy's rather then remarked, "Do you think mufflers grow on trees?"

Deep in thought, Billy imagines mufflers growing on trees. An entire orchard of them.

All night long the idea kept floating around in Billy's head. "A muffler tree."

As Billy prepared to go to sleep for the night, he asked his father, "Dad, is there really such a thing as a muffler tree?"

"Don't worry about it, son." said his father. "We'll get a new muffler for the car."

Billy goes to sleep and dreams about shopping at a garden supply store. He's at a seed rack where he surveys packets of seeds for planting. "Let's see, tomatoes, carrots, filters, spark plugs. Ah, mufflers!"

Billy purchases the muffler seeds and heads back home. In the garden at the back of the house he plants the seeds and waters them. As if by magic the seeds sprout and grow. And right in front of him a tree grows full of mufflers. Billy then picks a ripe one off the tree and takes it to his father's car. He removes the old, noisy one and installs his home-grown muffler on the car.

Billy then calls to his father, "Dad, I got your new muffler ready for you."

His father comes out and starts the car. There's a loud boom and a cloud of smoke at the back of the car.

Moral: Good mufflers don't grow on trees. They're only available at your Mydis dealer.

Some Last Words on the Subject

Over the course of two books and more than 200 tales I've presented to you much of my journey through life, including stories about family, friends, successes, and failures.

Based on feedback I received from readers of the first book, many have led parallel lives, had similar experiences, and interacted with some of the same people. Others have told me they've been inspired to write their own memoirs.

If I've brought a smile to your face and a laugh or lesson learned here and there, I'll consider this work a success.

Take the time to enjoy life and smell the roses, as it goes by very fast.

Made in the USA
Middletown, DE
16 July 2022

68999964R00129